THE ULTIMATE
CHICAGO BEARS
TRIVIA BOOK

A Collection of Amazing Trivia Quizzes
and Fun Facts for Die-Hard Bears Fans!

Ray Walker

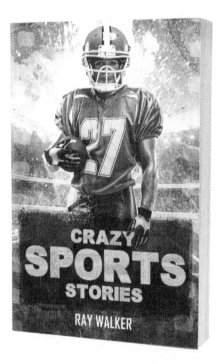

CONTENTS

INTRODUCTION

One of the two original NFL charter members still in existence, the Chicago Bears own a rich tapestry of history and success that spans nearly a century. From their humble beginnings in rural Illinois to the Monsters of the Midway, the Bears have always been one of the most feared and successful teams in the NFL. In this book, we explore that history in trivia form with 12 chapters chock-full of stories and facts about the Chicago Bears.

We will cover all of the eras in Bears history from George Halas and Red Grange through Mike Ditka and Dick Butkus all the way until Brian Urlacher and the present day. The Bears have seen so many of the best to ever play this game wear their jersey, that we're bound to miss out on some of your favorite facts about these stars. We will capture the many highs in Chicago's proud football history, and we might touch on some of the lows as well. But rest assured, this book will teach you about your favorite NFL franchise.

This book is designed to test the most die-hard Bears fans with trivia that will keep you on the edge of your seat. Each chapter in this book focuses on a specific topic of franchise history from specific positions to the record book. The chapters feature 20 multiple-choice or true-false questions, the answers to those questions, then 10 facts about the topic that sheds light on a random part of Bears history. Do not be alarmed if some of these questions stump you; the point of these questions is to help you learn more about your favorite team.

We hope you learn something new after devouring this book and use it to show off to your fellow Bears fans. All of the information conveyed in this book is current as of the beginning of the 2020 season, so things might have changed by the time you're reading this book. Now all that's left is to sit back, relax, and enjoy the hours of fun this book provides for the biggest Chicago Bears fans in the world.

CHAPTER 1:

ORIGINS & HISTORY

QUIZ TIME!

1. What was the franchise fee to join the American Professional Football Association in 1920, two years before the league renamed itself the National Football League?

    a. $100

    b. $250

    c. $500

    d. $1,000

2. In which season did the Chicago franchise win its first league championship?

    a. 1920

    b. 1921

    c. 1922

    d. 1923

3. Which of these famous firsts did the Chicago Bears NOT accomplish?

   a. Buy a player from another team
   b. Play in an indoor game
   c. Play in the first NFL championship game
   d. Play on national television

4. The Chicago Bears faced Washington in four consecutive NFL championship games from 1940 to 1943.

   a. True
   b. False

5. Who was NOT one of the coaches who replaced George Halas in between his four separate 10-year stints as Bears coach.

   a. Ralph Jones
   b. Paddy Driscoll
   c. Jim Dooley
   d. Hunk Anderson

6. What color did the Bears wear in the 1920 season because it matched with the Staley Starch Company, the team's sponsor for the first two seasons?

   a. Green
   b. Blue
   c. Gold
   d. Red

7. The Bears famously shared Wrigley Field with the Chicago Cubs from 1921 to 1970, and the "Friendly Confines"

unofficially holds the record for most NFL games hosted for a single franchise after the Bears played how many games on the North Side?

a. 324

b. 330

c. 335

d. 342

8. In which year did Chicago debut its trademark "C" logo on its helmets?

a. 1962

b. 1965

c. 1973

d. 1978

9. Which was the first decade without the Bears winning a championship?

a. 1930s

b. 1950s

c. 1960s

d. 1970s

10. Who was the Bears' first regular-season opponent as the home team at Soldier Field in 1971?

a. Green Bay Packers

b. Pittsburgh Steelers

c. Detroit Lions

d. Cleveland Browns

11. How many championships did George Halas win with the Bears?

    a. 4
    b. 5
    c. 6
    d. 7

12. Red Grange signed a $100,000 contract with the Chicago Bears for the 1925 season.

    a. True
    b. False

13. How many wins did the Bears have during their 19-game coast-to-coast tour with Red Grange in 1925?

    a. 6
    b. 9
    c. 11
    d. 13

14. The Monsters of the Midway moniker was first applied to which team?

    a. The 2006 Chicago Bears
    b. The 1985 Chicago Bears
    c. The 1963 Chicago Bears
    d. The 1940s Chicago Bears

15. Which of these coaches has NOT won 40 games as the Bears' coach?

    a. Dick Jauron
    b. Lovie Smith

c. Dave Wannstedt

d. George Halas

16. What was the nickname given to original Bears owner, coach, and general manager George Halas?

a. Bear Force One

b. Papa Bear

c. Big Bear

d. The Bearfather

17. Where did the Bears play in 2002 while Soldier Field was undergoing a renovation?

a. Northwestern's Ryan Field

b. Allstate Arena

c. University of Illinois's Memorial Stadium

d. Notre Dame Stadium

18. The Bears have more home wins since moving to Soldier Field than they had in 51 seasons at Wrigley Field.

a. True

b. False

19. Who did the Bears defeat in the "Walter Payton Game" just six days after the legend's death in 1999?

a. Green Bay Packers

b. Minnesota Vikings

c. Detroit Lions

d. St. Louis Rams

20. What is the relationship between current Bears chairman George H. McCaskey to founder George Halas?

a. No familial relationship
b. Son
c. Grandson
d. Great-grandson

QUIZ ANSWERS

1. A – $100

2. B – 1921

3. D – Play on national television

4. B – False

5. C – Jim Dooley

6. D – Red

7. B – 330

8. A – 1962

9. B – 1950s

10. B – Pittsburgh Steelers

11. C – 6

12. A – True

13. D – 13

14. D – The 1940s Chicago Bears

15. A – Dick Jauron

16. B – Papa Bear

17. C – University of Illinois's Memorial Stadium

18. B – False

19. A – Green Bay Packers

20. C – Grandson

DID YOU KNOW?

1. The Chicago Bears started as the Decatur Staleys, but that name lasted just one season before A.E. Staley asked George S. Halas to move the team to Chicago in order to match the popularity and profitability of baseball in the city. The agreement was that Staley would give Halas $5,000 to take over operations and run the team in Chicago, but the franchise had to keep the name for at least one year. Halas worked with Bill Veeck Sr. and William Wrigley to secure a lease to play at Cubs Park—which was later re-named Wrigley Field—and the rest is history. After that first year, Halas wanted to re-name the franchise the Chicago Cubs, but settled on the Bears because "I noted football players are much bigger players than baseball players, so if baseball players are cubs, then football players must be bears!"

2. The Bears started with red jerseys because it matched with the color scheme of the Staley Starch Company that sponsored the team, but once Halas was able to move the franchise to Chicago in 1921, the familiar blue and orange colors emerged. Halas based the color scheme on the University of Illinois, his alma mater, but the uniform colors really didn't become set until 1958 when the familiar patterns were first introduced. The Bears applied a white "C" to their helmets in 1962 and then

colored in that burnt orange in 1973, and it has barely changed over the last 40-plus years.

3. George Halas coached the Bears in four separate 10-year stints with a small break in between each tenure. He retired for the first time in 1930 and turned the coaching duties over to Ralph Jones, but Halas returned to the sidelines in 1933 and promptly led the Bears to the NFL championship. He enlisted in the Navy in 1942 during World War II, but again returned to lead Chicago to the title in 1946. He took another coaching sabbatical after the 1955 season, then returned for his final tenure as head coach in 1958. He finished his Bears career with 324 wins and just 151 losses, and he also coached in 31 ties with six championships to his name as a coach.

4. Ed Healey became the first player bought by another team in NFL history when the Bears paid $100 to the Rock Island Independents for Healey's contract. Healey was acquired almost immediately following Rock Island's game against the Bears in 1922 after Healey thoroughly dominated Chicago despite the Bears winning the game 3-0. Healey was actually very excited for the move because the Bears had far better amenities for their players than Rock Island provided. "At Rock Island, we had no showers and seldom a trainer. At Wrigley Field, we had a nice warm place to dress and nice warm showers."

5. Red Grange was a trendsetter for college football stars

when he made the jump to pro football in 1925 with the Chicago Bears. The original $100,000 contract covered a massive coast-to-coast barnstorming event that had the Bears play 19 games from November 26 until January 31 with just a two-week rest break in that stretch. Grange was limited to just 36 yards in his debut right after Thanksgiving, but he scored two touchdowns in Los Angeles in January to close the trip strong. Chicago went 13-5-1 on the trip, and Grange returned to the Bears from 1929 to 1934 after playing for the New York Yankees for two seasons following his initial year with the Bears.

6. The first NFL game played indoors also happened to be the first playoff game in league history. Before 1933, the league champion was decided based on the regular-season standings, but in 1932, Chicago tied with the Portsmouth Spartans for first place in the standings. Due to a blizzard and a subzero windchill in Chicago on December 18, 1932, the game was played at Chicago Stadium on a field that was only 80 yards long and 30 feet narrower than normal. The lone touchdown in the game came as Bronko Nagurski threw to Red Grange, and the Bears won the game 9-0.

7. The Chicago Bears' theme song, "Bear Down, Chicago Bears," has a unique history since being introduced in 1941. It was composed by Al Hoffman under the pseudonym Jerry Downs, and Hoffman didn't have an apparent connection to Chicago. The Russian-born composer is more well-known for his work on the original *Cinderella*

animated move for Disney. He is credited as a song writer for "Bibbidi-Bobbidi-Boo" and "A Dream Is a Wish Your Heart Makes" among the others.

8. In 1971, the Chicago Bears were forced to vacate Wrigley Field because the AFL-NFL merger required teams to play in stadiums that seated at least 50,000 fans. The Bears had hoped to originally play their games at Northwestern's Dyche Stadium, and actually played their first home game of the 1970 season at the home of the Wildcats, but a permanent move was blocked by Evanston residents and a Big Ten rule that professional sporting events not be played in on-campus stadiums. The Bears spent a lot of time looking for a new compliant home, and didn't settle on Soldier Field until May 1971, well after the NFL announced Chicago would host the Pittsburgh Steelers in the opening game. Soldier Field wasn't designed well for football, but it was the best of the options, which also included Comiskey Park and Arlington race track.

9. The only time the Bears have not designated Wrigley Field or Soldier Field as their home field since moving to Chicago was in 2002. The city signed off on a major renovation to Soldier Field in 2001 that would commence once the Bears' season ended in 2001. After Chicago lost to Philadelphia on January 19, 2002, in the NFC Divisional Round, demolition began inside the stadium, and the project lasted 20 months. The Bears fronted most of the cost for the Lakefront Improvement Plan with $224

million in support and an annual rent of $5.7 million. The rest of the funds were raised through a new hotel tax on hotels within city limits. The Bears opened the new stadium in 2003 on *Monday Night Football* against the rival Green Bay Packers, but lost the game 38-23.

10. Entering the 2020 season, the Bears had an NFL-record 769 wins in franchise history, 13 more than the rival Green Bay Packers. In 1997, the Bears defeated the Tampa Bay Buccaneers to become the first franchise to win 600 games. More than 11 years later, Chicago became the first team to win 700 games with a victory over the Jacksonville Jaguars.

CHAPTER 2:

NUMBERS GAME

QUIZ TIME!

1. What number did George Halas wear while he was a player-coach for the Bears from 1920 to 1929?

   a. 4

   b. 6

   c. 7

   d. 9

2. Which two numbers were retired by the Bears after just one player wearing them?

   a. 3 and 5

   b. 34 and 77

   c. 37 and 89

   d. 42 and 56

3. No one wore Gale Sayers's number 40 after he retired in 1971.

   a. True

   b. False

4. Who was the last player to wear number 51 for the Chicago Bears?

   a. Pat Fitzgerald
   b. Dick Butkus
   c. Mark Rodenhauser
   d. Bruce Herron

5. Which number was retired in honor of Brian Piccolo, who died of cancer in 1970?

   a. 38
   b. 41
   c. 47
   d. 49

6. Which of these players NEVER wore unlucky number 13 for the Bears?

   a. Allen Robinson
   b. Rick Mirer
   c. Rashad Ross
   d. Johnny Knox

7. For two seasons, Jared Allen hassled opposing quarterbacks wearing which number for the Bears?

   a. 75
   b. 73
   c. 71
   d. 69

8. Which number were so many teams chasing as they tried to hunt down Devin Hester on kickoff and punt returns?

a. 23

b. 24

c. 25

d. 27

9. Richard Dent was the first player to wear number 95 for the Chicago Bears.

a. True

b. False

10. Which number did Hall-of-Famer Orlando Pace wear during his one season in Chicago in 2009?

a. 74

b. 76

c. 78

d. 79

11. Which quarterback took over number 6 in Chicago for one season after Jay Cutler retired in 2016?

a. Mark Sanchez

b. Mike Glennon

c. Josh McCown

d. David Fales

12. Josh McCown wore number 12 at his first five stops in the NFL, but he had to wear number 15 for the Bears in 2011 because which other quarterback had that number when McCown joined the team?

a. Jimmy Clausen

b. Jordan Palmer

c. Caleb Hanie

d. Todd Collins

13. Which of these quarterbacks did NOT wear number 2 for the Bears during their stints in Chicago?

    a. Brian Hoyer

    b. Doug Flutie

    c. Jason Campbell

    d. Jimmy Clausen

14. How many players wore number 34 prior to Walter Payton donning the uniform number in 1975?

    a. 7

    b. 6

    c. 5

    d. 4

15. The Bears went more than 50 years without anyone wearing number 1 for the team.

    a. True

    b. False

16. Which cornerback with a delectable nickname wore number 33 for 12 seasons in Chicago?

    a. Gary Fencik

    b. Richie Petitbon

    c. Sherrick McManis

    d. Charles Tillman

17. Andy Frederick wore which number for three seasons before William Perry made it famous in Chicago from 1985 to 1993?

    a. 44
    b. 54
    c. 72
    d. 77

18. How long did it take between Mike Ditka leaving Chicago and his number 89 being retired by the Bears?

    a. 39 years
    b. 47 years
    c. 52 years
    d. 61 years

19. Which two numbers made their debut on a Bears player?

    a. 91 and 95
    b. 92 and 96
    c. 93 and 98
    d. 94 and 97

20. The Bears have retired more numbers than any other NFL franchise.

    a. True
    b. False

QUIZ ANSWERS

1. C – 7

2. D – 42 and 56

3. B – False

4. C – Mark Rodenhauser

5. B – 41

6. A – Allen Robinson

7. D – 69

8. A – 23

9. A – True

10. B – 76

11. A – Mark Sanchez

12. C – Caleb Hanie

13. D – Jimmy Clausen

14. A – 7

15. A – True

16. D – Charles Tillman

17. C – 72

18. B – 47 years

19. D – 94 and 97

20. A – True

DID YOU KNOW?

1. There are a handful of numbers that Bears have worn, but there are only two that only one player has ever worn for Chicago. The Bears retired Sid Luckman's number 42 and Bill Hewitt's number 56 before anyone else ever wore those numbers for the franchise. Luckman held most of the Bears' passing records prior to Jay Cutler and led Chicago to four NFL titles in his 12 seasons with the franchise. Hewitt played five years with the Bears and was one of the last players to not wear a helmet in the NFL.

2. In fact, the Bears have tended to take a long time to retire many numbers. Only five of the Bears' NFL-high 14 retired numbers were never re-issued after the honored player retired. Two of those five players received their honors posthumously, after dying while playing with the team. Chicago retired Willie Galimore's number 28 after he and teammate Bo Farrington died in 1964, just a few miles away from the team's training camp, when their car flipped on an Indiana road. Brian Piccolo's number 41 received the same treatment after he succumbed to cancer two years after Galimore's death. Walter Payton (34) is the fifth player whose number was officially taken out of circulation by the franchise before anyone else could wear it.

3. Jim Harbaugh's superstitious habits got the best of him after his rookie season with the Bears. He wore number 14 for Chicago after being a 1st round pick in the 1987 NFL Draft, but he struggled that season, including completing just one of 15 passes in a preseason game, and played in just six games as a backup. Frustrated with his performance and the results, Harbaugh switched to number 4, his number in college at Michigan, the following year and kept it for the rest of his career in Chicago.

4. Before Mitchell Trubisky wore number 10 for the Bears, it was worn by Milton Romney, who was a quarterback for Chicago from 1925 to 1929. Romney is the cousin of George Romney, a three-time governor in Michigan and the father of 2012 Republican Party presidential candidate Mitt Romney. In fact, Mitt is the current U.S. Senator's middle name, and he was named after the former Bears quarterback.

5. Khalil Mack's inspiration behind wearing the number 52 was Ray Lewis, the Hall of Fame linebacker who dominated on the field for Baltimore. Mack wore number 46 at college at the University at Buffalo because that was the grade the *NCAA Football* video game for EA Sports rated him as a freshman. But he could not wear that number in the NFL due to the numbering rules. He didn't hesitate in picking 52 to emulate his idol growing up.

6. The Bears have not officially retired number 50 for Mike Singletary, but only three players have worn the number since Singletary retired in 1992. It actually took 20 years

for Chicago to assign the uniform number to someone else, free-agent linebacker James Anderson, who wore the uniform for one season in 2013. Singletary was unaware that his number hadn't been worn by anyone else since his retirement, but chairman George McCaskey said Singletary told him, "I'd rather somebody wear it than see it hanging it up in a window somewhere."

7. Devin Hester exploited a loophole in the NFL rules to continue wearing number 23 after switching from cornerback to wide receiver. Hester was drafted as a cornerback and decided on the number 23 he wore in high school as his jersey number. He kept the number throughout his eight seasons in Chicago despite primarily playing wide receiver in addition to his returning duties. Once he left Chicago, however, the protections were lifted, and Hester was ineligible to wear number 23 without a position switch.

8. A July 2020 CBS Sports article listing the best players for every jersey number is littered with former Bears. Eleven of the 100 players listed spent at least one season with the Bears during their careers. Among those who spent their entire career in Chicago were Walter Payton representing number 34, Gale Sayers wearing number 40, Gary Fencik at number 45, Mike Singletary sporting number 50, and Dick Butkus for number 51. Some of the other honorees included Jay Cutler at number 6, Allen Page representing number 88, and Richard Dent being the choice for number 95.

9. On April 1, 2019, the Bears announced they would be wearing triple-digit uniform numbers in honor of the franchise's 100th season in the NFL. Each player would just tack on a "1" to the front of their jersey number, so quarterback Mitchell Trubisky was scheduled to wear number 110, and Khalil Mack was slated to don number 152. The plan was announced on Twitter with a video featuring chairman George H. McCaskey and Trubisky, talking about their thoughts on the concept and how they got NFL approval. Of course, the franchise later announced it was an April Fools' prank, but it was a clever one at that.

10. The Bears made a peculiar announcement in 2013 when it revealed it would retire Mike Ditka's number 89 that December. Chicago said it would no longer retire any jersey numbers, which coincided with Brian Urlacher announcing his retirement after a stellar 13-year career with the Bears. Of course, nothing prevents the Bears from not issuing the jersey number to anyone, as no one has worn number 54 since Urlacher's retirement, but the Hall-of-Famer won't get his special midfield moment for a jersey retirement any time soon.

CHAPTER 3:

CALLING THE SIGNALS

QUIZ TIME!

1. How many consecutive years did Sid Luckman throw for 1,000 yards as the Bears rolled through the NFL in the 1940s?

    a. 9

    b. 8

    c. 7

    d. 6

2. How long did Sid Luckman hold the single-season passing yards record before it was broken?

    a. 15 years

    b. 20 years

    c. 25 years

    d. 30 years

3. Which Bears quarterback has won the most games as Chicago's starter since the stat was first kept in 1950?

    a. Kyle Orton

b. Rex Grossman

c. Jim McMahon

d. Jay Cutler

4. In which season did Sid Luckman win his only MVP award?

   a. 1941

   b. 1943

   c. 1945

   d. 1947

5. How many times have Bears quarterbacks thrown for at least 20 passing touchdowns?

   a. 10

   b. 12

   c. 15

   d. 19

6. When was the last time the Bears' leading passer in a season had fewer than 1,000 yards?

   a. 1968

   b. 1986

   c. 1997

   d. 2004

7. How many passes did Mitchell Trubisky throw in 2019 when he set the Bears' record for most pass attempts in a game without throwing an interception?

   a. 48

   b. 51

c. 54

d. 57

8. Which team has allowed the most 300-yard passing performances to Bears quarterbacks?

    a. Minnesota Vikings

    b. Detroit Lions

    c. New York Giants

    d. Green Bay Packers

9. Sid Luckman still holds the record for the most passes intercepted in a single season.

    a. True

    b. False

10. How many quarterbacks have the Bears drafted in the 1st round?

    a. 7

    b. 8

    c. 9

    d. 10

11. Which Bears record does Erik Kramer NOT hold?

    a. Most touchdown passes in a season

    b. Most passing attempts in a game

    c. Most passing yards in a game

    d. Most passing yards in a season

12. Sid Luckman was the first quarterback in NFL history to pass for 400 yards in a game.

a. True

b. False

13. What was Jay Cutler's career completion percentage with the Bears?

    a. 62.6

    b. 63.1

    c. 60.3

    d. 61.8

14. Cade McNown was supposed to be the Bears' answer at quarterback when they drafted him with the 12th pick of the 1st round in 1999. How many games did he end up starting for Chicago before they traded him?

    a. 13

    b. 15

    c. 17

    d. 19

15. The Bears have never lost a game in which their quarterback has thrown for 400 yards.

    a. True

    b. False

16. Since 1961, the most starting quarterbacks the Bears have had in a single season is five in 1984. Who did NOT start a game for Chicago that year?

    a. Vince Evans

    b. Steve Fuller

    c. Bob Avellini

    d. Greg Landry

17. Jim McMahon's best statistical season came during the 1985 Super Bowl season when he threw for how many yards?

   a. 2,392
   b. 2,467
   c. 2,598
   d. 2,702

18. Which television network did Jay Cutler sign with after being cut by the Bears and retiring?

   a. CBS
   b. NFL Network
   c. FOX
   d. ESPN

19. How many touchdown passes did Jay Cutler throw for the Bears in his career to set the franchise record?

   a. 137
   b. 143
   c. 154
   d. 162

20. Who was the starting quarterback on Chicago's 1963 NFL championship team?

   a. Larry Rakestraw
   b. Ed Brown
   c. Rudy Bukich
   d. Bill Wade

QUIZ ANSWERS

1. B – 8

2. A – 15 years

3. D – Jay Cutler

4. B – 1943

5. B – 12

6. D – 2004

7. C – 54

8. B – Detroit Lions

9. A – True

10. C – 9

11. C – Most passing yards in a game

12. A – True

13. D – 61.8

14. B – 15

15. B – False

16. A – Vince Evans

17. A – 2,392

18. C – FOX

19. C – 154

20. D – Bill Wade

DID YOU KNOW?

1. Sid Luckman's football career was taking off at the same time his personal life was crumbling behind the scenes. During Luckman's freshman year at Columbia, his father and two accomplices were convicted of murder in a court case that dominated the headlines. The attention and situation almost caused Luckman to drop out of Columbia, but Lou Little, Columbia's football coach at the time, convinced his quarterback to stay in school. Two years later, Luckman was the talk of the nation after leading Columbia to an upset win over Army, and then he was picked by the Bears in the 1939 NFL Draft.

2. In the aftermath of Chicago's lopsided win over Washington in the NFL title game, Luckman enlisted as a volunteer ensign with the U.S. Merchant Marines. He worked out an agreement that would allow him to play the 1944 and 1945 seasons with the Bears, but he was not allowed to practice during the week with the team. Luckman started just twice and appeared in 17 games for the Bears over those two seasons, but he returned in 1946 to lead the Bears to another championship, and he set a career high in 1947 with 2,712 passing yards.

3. Bill Wade is one of the best quarterbacks in Bears history, but is largely forgotten in the grand scheme of things because he predated the Super Bowl era. Wade led

Chicago to the NFL championship in 1963 and ran for both touchdowns in the Bears' 14-10 win over the Giants. He was the 1951 SEC Player of the Year and was the president of his freshman class at Vanderbilt. Wade suffered from some health challenges later in life and was blind for many of his final years of life before he died in 2016. Ironically, he died nine days after Rudy Bukich, who was the backup quarterback on that 1963 championship team.

4. Johnny Lujack's post-career was almost as fascinating as the career he had on the field for the Bears. He started out on defense because Luckman was still at the helm of Chicago's T-formation offense, but then replaced Luckman as the starter the following year in 1949. He surprised everyone by retiring at 26 years old to take a job coaching at Notre Dame, but once he was passed over for the head coach job at his alma mater, he quit coaching. Instead, Lujack sold cars and built the biggest Chevy dealership between Chicago and Des Moines in Davenport, Iowa.

5. Jim McMahon is well-known for being the quarterback on the famous 1985 Bears team that romped to the Super Bowl. But the beating he took in his 15 years in the NFL has had an adverse reaction on his health now that he's retired. The multiple concussions he suffered in his career have left him with depression, migraines, other debilitating pain, as well as early-onset dementia. He said the use of medical marijuana has been a "godsend" for him in terms of dealing with the pain, and has helped regulate his life more since retirement.

6. Many would assume that McMahon's public appearances with sunglasses are related to his health struggle. However, the reason behind the sunglasses predates his entire football career. In 2018, McMahon clarified the rumors around his sunglasses in a tweet. He said the eye injury came from playing "Cowboys and Indians" with his brother, and he tried to untie the knot on the holster of his toy gun with a fork. The fork slipped, and two of the tines went through his eye.

7. Erik Kramer had a long road to becoming the Bears' starter for four seasons in the 1990s. He wasn't heavily recruited in high school in California, so he attended Pierce Junior College. He was looking for some place to transfer, and ended up at North Carolina State, mostly because the Wolfpack had just won the NCAA Division I basketball title. After going undrafted in 1987, he joined the Atlanta Falcons as a replacement player during the strike, but when the strike ended, he headed to the Canadian Football League. He tore a ligament in his knee in 1989 while in Canada, and he didn't want to return, so he sent out feelers to the NFL, and the Lions brought him in for a workout in 1990. He signed a big deal with Chicago in 1994, and he threw for 3,000 yards in both 1995 and 1997 before Chicago moved on.

8. Rex Grossman might be one of two Chicago quarterbacks to start a Super Bowl for the Bears, but that has not prevented him from getting his fair share of criticism. In fact, he was named the worst starting quarterback of the 63

who have started a Super Bowl through 2020 by NFL.com. The author noted that Grossman only had three seasons in which he started more than three games, which is fair, and Grossman's 2006 stats weren't stellar. In leading Chicago to a 13-3 record in 2006, Grossman completed just 54.6% of his passes and threw 23 touchdowns compared to 20 interceptions.

9. Jay Cutler's time in Chicago might be considered a disappointment because the Bears had just two winning seasons and made the playoffs just once in his eight seasons with the team. However, Cutler will go down as the best statistical quarterback in franchise history, even if he wasn't the championship answer. He holds the team record for almost every major statistical category, including passing attempts, completions, and touchdown passes. Depending upon how the Mitchell Trubisky era ends with the Bears, Cutler might also end up leading in completion percentage and quarterback rating as well.

10. Mitchell Trubisky earned the nickname "Mr. Biscuit" as a freshman at North Carolina thanks to a mumbling friend. As he told the *New York Post* ahead of the 2017 NFL Draft, he was having dinner with one of his coaches, their wife, and a family friend, and one of them stumbled over his name while talking. What came out sounded like "Mr. Biscuit," and by the next week at practice, the moniker stuck with his Tar Heels teammates.

CHAPTER 4:

BETWEEN THE TACKLES

QUIZ TIME!

1. Which of these running backs NEVER ran for 200 yards in a game for the Bears?

   a. Gale Sayers

   b. Walter Payton

   c. Matt Forte

   d. Thomas Jones

2. Who holds the NFL record among running backs for the highest average gain per carry in a season?

   a. Red Grange

   b. Beattie Feathers

   c. Gale Sayers

   d. Bobby Douglass

3. Which of these running backs does NOT share the Bears' record with four rushing touchdowns in a game?

   a. Bobby Douglass

   b. Gale Sayers

c. Rick Casares

d. Walter Payton

4. How many times have the Bears had two 100-yard rushers in the same game?

    a. 2

    b. 3

    c. 4

    d. 5

5. The Bears have lost as many games in which Walter Payton ran for 100 yards as Matt Forte ran for 100 yards with Chicago.

    a. True

    b. False

6. Walter Payton led the NFC in rushing five times, but how many times did he lead the NFL in rushing yards?

    a. 1

    b. 2

    c. 3

    d. 4

7. What event prevented Walter Payton from rushing for 1,000 yards in 1982, interrupting a streak that would have been 11 consecutive years?

    a. Blizzard

    b. Players' strike

    c. Knee injury

    d. Suspension

8. How many times did Walter Payton rush for multiple touchdowns in a game?

    a. 18
    b. 21
    c. 24
    d. 27

9. Walter Payton has twice as many yards as the second-place rusher in Bears history.

    a. True
    b. False

10. Since Walter Payton's retirement in 1987, which running back has NOT led the Bears in scoring during a season?

    a. Neal Anderson
    b. Thomas Jones
    c. Jordan Howard
    d. Matt Forte

11. How much daylight did Gale Sayers famously say he needed?

    a. 1 yard
    b. 40 centimeters
    c. 2 feet
    d. 18 inches

12. What didn't Gale Sayers accomplish as a rookie in his first preseason game with the Bears?

    a. 57-yard rushing touchdown
    b. 77-yard punt return touchdown

c. 25-yard touchdown pass

d. 93-yard kickoff return touchdown

13. How many yards did Gale Sayers rush for in his Bears career?

a. 4,765

b. 5,198

c. 5,072

d. 4,956

14. How many years did Neal Anderson lead the Bears in rushing?

a. 5

b. 6

c. 7

d. 8

15. Cedric Benson was the last running back the Bears have drafted in the first two rounds.

a. True

b. False

16. What was Red Grange's legal first name?

a. Harold

b. Ronald

c. Reginald

d. Humphrey

17. Matt Forte set an NFL record in 2014 for most receptions by a running back. How many catches did he have for the Bears that season?

a. 93

b. 97

c. 99

d. 102

18. No NFL player had more yards from scrimmage during Matt Forte's eight seasons in Chicago than Forte's 12,718 for the Bears.

a. True

b. False

19. In which season did the Bears set a 16-game low for rushing yards in a season with just 1,330 yards?

a. 1999

b. 2007

c. 1994

d. 2016

20. How many Bears running backs are enshrined in the Hall of Fame?

a. 3

b. 5

c. 6

d. 7

QUIZ ANSWERS

1. D – Thomas Jones
2. B – Beattie Feathers
3. D – Walter Payton
4. C – 4
5. A – True
6. A – 1
7. B – Players' strike
8. C – 24
9. B – False
10. B – Thomas Jones
11. D – 18 inches
12. A – 57-yard rushing touchdown
13. D – 4,956
14. C – 7
15. B – False
16. A – Harold
17. D – 102
18. A – True
19. B – 2007
20. C – 6

DID YOU KNOW?

1. Old footage of Red Grange's first game with the Bears was discovered in 1997 by the McKearnan family as they were clearing old boxes belonging to their late father. They started to watch some old 16-milimeter films and noticed how pictures of a family vacation changed to this raucous stadium atmosphere. More than two decades later, when the siblings wanted to convert the films to digital, they recognized Red Grange's face on the screen. They contacted the Bears, who authenticated it as the Thanksgiving Day game in 1925 against the Chicago Cardinals at Wrigley Field, and the franchise now owns the video for their archives.

2. Bronko Nagurski is known now as the namesake of a college football award for the best defensive player in the country, but he excelled at running back as well for the Bears during his playing career. He led Chicago in rushing in 1933, then again in 1936, and finished his career with more than 2,700 rushing yards over nine years with the Bears. He retired before the 1938 season because he couldn't get a raise from the Bears and became a pro wrestler, but he didn't stay away from the gridiron forever. With the Bears short on bodies due to World War II, Nagurski returned to Chicago in 1943 as a tackle, but switched to fullback later in the season with Chicago needing him to again be a tough, physical

runner. His runs helped the Bears reach the 1943 NFL championship game against Washington, and he finished his career with the rushing touchdown that ultimately won the Bears the title that season.

3. On November 30, 1971, *Brian's Song*, the television movie that depicts the friendship between Bears Hall of Fame running back Gale Sayers and teammate Brian Piccolo, was first aired on ABC. The film was based on Sayers's autobiography, *I Am Third*, and stars James Caan as Piccolo and Billy Dee Williams as Sayers. The pair were roommates with the Bears in 1967, the first time an NFL team had interracial roommates, and the two developed a close bond. Piccolo played a key role in helping Sayers rehabilitate from a knee injury in 1968, so when Sayers was honored with the George S. Halas Award in 1969 as the most courageous player in professional football, he wanted to bring Piccolo and give him the award. Instead, Piccolo had just finished treatment for testicular cancer, so Sayers gave the speech that became the centerpiece of the 73-minute movie.

4. Gale Sayers's post-football careers were just as successful as Sayers's brief but electrifying career on the field. He was the athletics director for five years at Southern Illinois University's flagship campus in Carbondale, and tripled the donations to the school's athletics department in his tenure. He quit his job there to start Crest Computer Supply Co. in 1984, a business that grew to be worth more than $100 million and was renamed Sayers40, Inc. The

company is still offering IT services to more than 400 clients, including several in the Fortune 500. He also supported and founded several philanthropic endeavors in Chicago and its suburbs, notably the Cradle Foundation. The foundation established the Gale Sayers Center in the Austin neighborhood of Chicago to service underprivileged youths through afterschool programs.

5. There are conflicting sources as to how Walter Payton acquired his signature "Sweetness" nickname in college at Jackson State. The first is that it naturally summarized his athletic ability in general. The second was closely related; it was simply a description of Payton's running style. The third one is it had to do with the kindness and respect Payton showed to others, which will ultimately be his legacy in the league. Every year, the NFL awards the Walter Payton Man of the Year Award to a player "for his excellence on and off the field." Each NFL team nominates one player per season who had made a significant impact in their local community for the award. Payton actually won the award himself in 1977 — before it was renamed in his honor after his death in 1999 — and Charles Tillman in 2013 is the only Bears player to win the award since its rededication.

6. Neal Anderson is one of the most underrated players in Bears history largely because of the man he replaced. Anderson was a 1st round pick in 1986, knowing full well he was going to be the successor to Walter Payton. He was not as dynamic or explosive as Payton, but

Anderson still made four Pro Bowls and steadied the Bears' rushing attack after Payton's retirement. In his post-football life, Anderson runs a peanut farm in Gainesville, Florida, and helped found and run the Community Bank and Trust of Florida, which had 11 branches in three counties as of 2014.

7. Thomas Jones had a very productive career with five NFL teams, but he made his mark originally with the Bears. He had his first two of five consecutive 1,000-yard seasons with Chicago after rushing for 948 yards in his first season with Chicago. Nowadays, he's added his middle initial, Q, to his name and has become an actor. Most people probably know him for his role of Comanche on Netflix's *Luke Cage*, but he has also appeared in the recent *Hawaii Five-O* reboot on CBS, as well as the feature film *Straight Outta Compton*.

8. Cedric Benson is arguably the biggest draft bust in Bears history after a disastrous three-year career in Chicago. The 4th overall pick in 2005 ran only 1,593 yards on 420 carries for the Bears, but could not seem to stay out of trouble off the field. He held out for most of his first preseason before signing a week or so before the opening game. The breaking point, though, came right before the 2008 season when he was arrested twice for alcohol-related crimes in the span of roughly a month, and the Bears subsequently released him.

9. Matt Forte was part of the revolutionary class of running backs that made an impact both as a runner and a

receiver for teams. But nobody did it better than Forte, who was the definition of an every-down back for the Bears for eight seasons. He caught at least 50 passes in six of his years in Chicago, with a low mark of 44 receptions in 2012 and 2015 and that record of 102 in 2014. He also had five 1,000-yard rushing seasons and was named to the Pro Bowl twice. In his 10 years in the league, including those final two with the Jets, no one had as many touches (2,910) or yards from scrimmage (14,468) as Forte did during his career.

10. Former Bears running back Jordan Howard wore the same white shirt under his jersey in every game he's played since his father died in 2007. The shirt is pretty beaten up by this point, but it features a photo of his dad smiling along with the words, "In memory of my Dad, "Doc" Reginald Howard." Howard said the shirt helps him feel like his father is always with him, especially now that he is living his dream of playing in the NFL.

CHAPTER 5:

CATCHING THE BALL

QUIZ TIME!

1. Walter Payton leads the Bears in total receptions, so which receiver ranks second on the all-time list?

   a. Marty Booker

   b. Brandon Marshall

   c. Johnny Morris

   d. Curtis Conway

2. Who caught the longest touchdown pass in Bears history?

   a. Johnny Knox

   b. John Farrington

   c. Devin Hester

   d. Bobby Engram

3. How many times did Mike Ditka lead the Bears in receiving yards during his career?

   a. 3

   b. 2

   c. 5

   d. 4

4. What is Ken Kavanaugh's franchise record for most yards per catch in a career?

   a. 20.9 yards
   b. 21.2 yards
   c. 21.8 yards
   d. 22.4 yards

5. In which year did Johnny Morris become the only Bears receiver to lead the NFL in receiving yards and lead the league in receptions?

   a. 1961
   b. 1962
   c. 1963
   d. 1964

6. How many times have the Bears had a receiver go over 1,000 yards receiving in a season?

   a. 14
   b. 16
   c. 18
   d. 20

7. Which of these talented receivers NEVER had two 1,000-yard seasons for the Bears?

   a. Jeff Graham
   b. Marty Booker
   c. Curtis Conway
   d. Brandon Marshall

8. Who was the first Bears receiver to catch 100 passes in a season?

   a. Harlon Hill
   b. Brandon Marshall
   c. Marty Booker
   d. Johnny Morris

9. Before Alshon Jeffery broke the single-game record for receiving yards twice in 2013, who held the Bears' record for most receiving yards in a game?

   a. Johnny Morris
   b. Brandon Marshall
   c. Harlon Hill
   d. Marty Booker

10. Brandon Marshall holds the Bears' record with 15 100-yard games in his Chicago career.

    a. True
    b. False

11. In 1999, Marcus Robinson led the Bears in receiving yards and scoring, but his 84 receptions were four fewer than which Chicago receiver?

    a. Bobby Engram
    b. Curtis Conway
    c. Eddie Kennison
    d. Ricky Proehl

12. Marty Booker holds the Bears' record for most consecutive games with a catch at 60 games, but that

streak spans his two tenures with the team. How long was the steak in 2004 when he was traded to the Miami Dolphins?

   a. 52 games

   b. 54 games

   c. 56 games

   d. 58 games

13. What is the Bears' record, shared by four receivers, for most 100-yard receiving games in a season?

   a. 5

   b. 6

   c. 7

   d. 8

14. Brandon Marshall had a large impact in Chicago over the course of his three years with the team, but how many times did he lead the Bears in receiving yards?

   a. 3

   b. 2

   c. 1

   d. 0

15. In which season did Devin Hester tie the NFL record for punt return touchdowns with four?

   a. 2007

   b. 2006

   c. 2008

   d. 2005

16. Mike Ditka was the Rookie of the Year in 1961 after catching 56 passes and eclipsing 1,000 yards.

    a. True
    b. False

17. How many catches did Mike Ditka have in 1964 when he set the NFL record for most receptions in a season by a tight end?

    a. 73
    b. 75
    c. 78
    d. 82

18. Mike Ditka was the first person to win a Super Bowl as both a player and a head coach.

    a. True
    b. False

19. Harlon Hill became the namesake of the trophy awarded to the best player in which NCAA division?

    a. Football Bowl Subdivision
    b. Football Championship Subdivision
    c. Division II
    d. Division III

20. Allen Robinson II set a pair of Chicago postseason records with his performance in the NFC Wild Card game in 2019. How many receptions and receiving yards did Robinson have that day against Philadelphia?

a. 10 catches, 143 yards
b. 11 catches, 157 yards
c. 10 catches, 171 yards
d. 12 catches, 129 yards

QUIZ ANSWERS

1. C – Johnny Morris

2. B – John Farrington

3. A – 3

4. D – 22.4 yards

5. D – 1964

6. B – 16

7. A – Jeff Graham

8. C – Marty Booker

9. C – Harlon Hill

10. B – False

11. A – Bobby Engram

12. D – 58 games

13. C – 7

14. C – 1

15. A – 2007

16. A – True

17. B – 75

18. B – False

19. C – Division II

20. A – 10 catches, 143 yards

DID YOU KNOW?

1. Harlon Hill earned plenty of hardware during his time in Chicago playing for the Bears. He was named the NFL's Rookie of the Year in 1954 after catching 45 passes for 1,124 yards and 12 touchdowns. The following year, he was the inaugural winner of the Jim Thorpe Trophy given to the NFL's most valuable player, and earned his first of consecutive All-Pro selections. He was named to the Pro Bowl in each of his first three seasons in the league after leading the league in receiving touchdowns in each of his first two years.

2. Ken Kavanaugh was unaware that the Bears even drafted him out of LSU in 1940. He originally signed with Branch Rickey and the St. Louis Cardinals as a minor-league first baseman for $300 per month. When he learned the Bears had drafted him, George Halas offered Kavanaugh $50 per game to play for Chicago. After some negotiation, Kavanaugh worked Halas up to $300 per game, and he switched sports to play in Chicago. At the time of his death in 2007, Kavanaugh owned or shared four franchise records from his eight seasons with the team.

3. Dick Gordon and Bears management had a series of very public disputes as the receiver's career began to explode on the field. The two sides battled almost every year over his contract and other issues such as his wardrobe and hairstyle. After his career year in 1970, in which he led

53

the league with 71 catches and 13 touchdowns, he threatened to not play in games unless he received more money despite practicing with the team. Eventually, Gordon made comments in 1971 that angered George Halas enough to "trade" him to the Rams in 1972 using the Rozelle Rule of free agency. Gordon was also a major part of the group of players that eventually had the Rozelle Rule overturned in federal court in 1976.

4. Willie Gault was known for his blazing speed on the football field, and that hasn't gone away as he's aged and focused on acting. In 2016, Gault set world records in the 100- and 200-meter dashes for men 55 years old or older, having already set records in the 45-49-year-old age bracket and the 50-54-year-old age bracket. Gault famously qualified for the 1980 U.S. Olympics track team that boycotted the Summer Games in Moscow, Russia, but he was part of the 4x100-meter relay team that set a world record at the 1983 World Championships before he even played a game for the Bears.

5. Curtis Conway might be well known in Chicago for his contributions to the Bears over his seven years with the team, but he still has a long way to go to match the fame of his wife. Conway married boxing champion Laila Ali, the daughter of Muhammed Ali, in July 2007, and the couple have two children in addition to Conway's three children from a previous marriage. The two met at a small party Conway hosted in 2005, and the two were engaged on Thanksgiving 2006.

6. After moving on from the Bears in 2000, Bobby Engram had a productive career in Seattle. However, he was almost forced to retire in 2006 due to a thyroid condition that left him fatigued to the point that it affected his everyday life. He missed a good chunk of the 2006 season—ironically enough, his final game before being diagnosed was in Chicago against the Bears—with an accelerated heart rate, the fatigue and weight loss. The cause was a virus and a diagnosis of Grave's Disease, a thyroid condition that causes the body to attack the thyroid. Engram spent two months in treatment to build back up his strength, and he returned for the final three games of the 2006 season before catching seven passes for 120 yards in the postseason.

7. Marty Booker had an interesting superstition for game days, one that got the normally cerebral receiver a little animated on game day. Booker wears a rubber band on his left wrist, which isn't a big deal until one day when his bag of rubber bands went missing on game day. He told ESPN that he was panicking and cursed out the locker room attendants as they scrambled to search for the rubber bands. It turns out that everyone had to shift down a locker for some reason, and Booker's rubber bands were in the locker next to his. He said it started in college when he had a good game while wearing the rubber band, and the superstition spread quickly.

8. Devin Hester played cornerback during his time at Miami, and he was drafted by the Bears with the

expectations he would play in the defensive backfield. But with the Bears struggling to find offensive weapons entering the 2007 season, coach Lovie Smith made the move to switch Hester to offense and hopefully get the ball in his hands more. He had more than 50 catches in 2008 and 2009, but otherwise, the six-year experiment was kind of a failure. He made 217 catches for 2,807 yards and 14 touchdowns in his time at receiver for the Bears, which ultimately fell short of the expectations for the dynamic playmaker.

9. In 2017, Brandon Marshall wrote a column for The Players' Tribune about his struggles with borderline personality disorder, which he was diagnosed with in 2011. That same year, he started Project 375 with his wife, Michi, as a platform for him to advocate for mental health and try to end the stigma around mental health disorders. The column was another avenue to dispel the myths around mental health disorder as he wrote about his experiences with being diagnosed with a mental health disorder and going through three months of outpatient treatment in Massachusetts. He wrote in the column that he journals every day and tries to share his story as much as possible to raise awareness and inspire people to get help.

10. Alshon Jeffery's tenure in Chicago ended a little choppy over the final two seasons. He missed almost half of the 2015 season with injuries, yet still led the Bears in 54 catches and 807 yards in just nine games. The following

year, he was suspended for four games for use of performance-enhancing drugs, a positive test Jeffery blamed on a supplement meant to combat inflammation. Jeffery was the team's leading receiver at the time of the suspension, but he was not re-signed after the 2016 season and ended up signing with Philadelphia.

CHAPTER 6:

TRENCH WARFARE

QUIZ TIME!

1. Which offensive lineman appeared in the most Pro Bowls representing the Bears?

    a. Olin Kreutz

    b. Ruben Brown

    c. Jay Hilgenberg

    d. Bill George

2. The first four Pro Bowl selections the Bears had were all offensive linemen.

    a. True

    b. False

3. Which long snapper holds the Bears' record with 16 seasons played with the team?

    a. Doug Buffone

    b. George Trafton

    c. Patrick Mannelly

    d. Olin Kreutz

4. Which center finished one game shy of Walter Payton's franchise record for most games started with the Bears?

   a. Clyde "Bulldog" Turner
   b. Mike Pyle
   c. Olin Kreutz
   d. Dan Neal

5. How many members of the 1942 Bears offensive line that paved the way for Chicago to go 11-0 in the regular season were named First Team All-Pros after the season?

   a. 4
   b. 3
   c. 2
   d. 1

6. Stan Jones is considered one of the first professional football players to use which type of exercise to get into shape for the season?

   a. Weightlifting
   b. Marathon running
   c. Mountain climbing
   d. Cross-training

7. How much did the Bears guarantee George Connor per season in his first contract with the team, a high salary for an offensive lineman at the time?

   a. $10,000
   b. $11,000
   c. $12,000
   d. $13,000

8. An offensive lineman holds the record for most consecutive games played for the Bears.

    a. True
    b. False

9. Who was the last Bears offensive lineman to be named a First Team All-Pro selection?

    a. Bill George
    b. Olin Kreutz
    c. Jay Hilgenberg
    d. Jimbo Covert

10. Which two Bears linemen made an appearance at WrestleMania 2 as part of the NFL stars brought in to wrestle Andre the Giant?

    a. Jay Hilgenberg and William "Refrigerator" Perry
    b. Steve McMichael and Richard Dent
    c. Jimbo Covert and William "Refrigerator" Perry
    d. Jimbo Covert and Richard Dent

11. Richard Dent led the Bears in sacks eight of the 10 seasons between 1984 and 1993. Which defensive lineman led Chicago the other two seasons?

    a. Steve McMichael
    b. William Perry
    c. Dan Hampton
    d. Trace Armstrong

12. Richard Dent is the only Bears player to ever record 15 sacks in a season.

a. True

b. False

13. Richard Dent set the Bears' record for sacks in a game in 1984, then he tied it three years later. Ironically, those two performances came against the same opponent. Which team was Dent facing when he set, then tied the record?

    a. New York Jets
    b. Detroit Lions
    c. Dallas Cowboys
    d. Los Angeles Raiders

14. Who is the Bears' leader in career fumble recoveries?

    a. Julius Peppers
    b. Brian Urlacher
    c. Dick Butkus
    d. Steve McMichael

15. Bill George is largely credited as being the first player to line up at which now standard position?

    a. Nose guard
    b. Nickel back
    c. Long snapper
    d. Middle linebacker

16. Who holds Chicago's record for most consecutive games with a sack?

    a. Rosevelt Colvin
    b. Mark Anderson
    c. Richard Dent
    d. Khalil Mack

17. Which of these famous Bears defenders was twice named the Associated Press NFL Defensive Player of the Year?

    a. Mike Singletary
    b. Dick Butkus
    c. Brian Urlacher
    d. Richard Dent

18. How many consecutive years was Mike Singletary named a First Team All-Pro linebacker?

    a. 7
    b. 6
    c. 5
    d. 4

19. Brian Urlacher led the Bears in sacks at least once during his career.

    a. True
    b. False

20. Khalil Mack made an instant impact on the field for the Bears after arriving from the Raiders. What didn't Mack do in his first game with Chicago?

    a. Recover a fumble
    b. Record a sack
    c. Score a touchdown
    d. Lead the team in tackles

QUIZ ANSWERS

1. D – Bill George

2. A – True

3. C – Patrick Mannelly

4. C – Olin Kreutz

5. B – 3

6. A – Weightlifting

7. D – $13,000

8. B – False

9. B – Olin Kreutz

10. C – Jimbo Covert and William "Refrigerator" Perry

11. A – Steve McMichael

12. B – False

13. D – Los Angeles Raiders

14. C – Dick Butkus

15. D – Middle linebacker

16. A – Rosevelt Colvin

17. A – Mike Singletary

18. B – 6

19. A – True

20. D – Lead the team in tackles

DID YOU KNOW?

1. Bill George became the first middle linebacker, and it paid dividends for him almost instantly. He arrived in Chicago to play middle guard (what would be called nose guard in modern-day football), but in a 1954 game against the Eagles, he was frustrated by the short passes Philadelphia was completing over his head. His normal job at passing play was to bump the center before dropping back in coverage, but he began just dropping straight back instead. Two plays after making that decision, he intercepted the first of 18 passes in his career, beginning the development of the modern-day middle linebacker.

2. Roy "Link" Lyman was a born winner during his football career. He had just one losing season in 16 years of playing high school, college, and professional football. He's probably most well-known for originating the shifts and constant motion of the defense in modern-day professional football. Lyman routinely slid and shifted around along the defensive line to help confuse opponents. He said he tried to disguise his movements in order to fool his blocker and make it easier to make the tackle. His ability to read and diagnose plays allowed him to perfectly time his jumps and get an edge on most of his defenders.

3. George Connor definitely was not destined to be an offensive lineman when he was born in 1921. He was

born two months premature and weighed less than three pounds, giving him less than a 10% chance of surviving. His mother was a nurse and fed him a diet of boiled cabbage every hour for a year to help him build up strength. He grew up to be 6-foot-3 and 240 pounds and played on both lines for Holy Cross and Notre Dame before the Bears drafted him. Chicago eventually moved him to linebacker to help defend against sweeps, but the fact he even played football is a minor miracle.

4. The Bears have the Detroit Lions to thank for Clyde "Bulldog" Turner joining the team. College scouting was far from the system it would be just 20 or 30 years later, and teams still relied on preseason magazines to help their scouting in the 1930s. That meant players at small colleges, like Turner at Hardin-Simmons, were often overlooked. A fan of Hardin-Simmons notified Bears scout Frank Korch about Turner's ability, and after seeing Turner play, Korch convinced George Halas to draft Turner in 1940. The Lions were the only other team to heavily scout and pursue Turner, but Detroit was so convinced no one else was onto Turner and that he would sign with them as a free agent that the Lions never drafted him.

5. George Musso had the golden chance to run over not one but two U.S. presidents during his football career. While playing at Millikin College (now Millikin University) in Decatur, Illinois, Musso lined up against Eureka College, who had an offensive guard named Ronald Reagan.

65

Years later, when the Bears played the College All-Stars as the defending NFL champions, the center on that team was Michigan's Gerald Ford.

6. Dan Fortmann was already thinking about his next stage of life while playing for the Chicago Bears. He enrolled at the University of Chicago medical school in 1936, the same year he was drafted by the Bears, and he graduated with his degree in 1940. He still played for Chicago until 1943 when he joined the Navy and was stationed on a hospital ship in the Pacific Ocean. He eventually became the team doctor of the Los Angeles Rams while practicing surgery in southern California.

7. Steve McMichael certainly had a unique life after retiring from the NFL in 1994. He joined World Championship Wrestling in 1995, and was inducted into the legendary Four Horsemen in 1996 before the group was disbanded a year later. It was in 1997 when he won the WCW United States Heavyweight Championship over Jeff Jarrett. He later coached the Chicago Slaughter of the Continental Indoor Football League from 2007 to 2013, winning a championship with the team in 2009. He also ran for mayor in Romeoville, Illinois, in 2013 and was defeated by the incumbent.

8. Mike Singletary's coaching career was far from the success he had as a player. However, Singletary will always be remembered for one of the most memorable rants in the twenty-first century. Singletary sent Vernon

Davis to the locker room in the fourth quarter of a 2008 game when Singletary was the interim coach of the San Francisco 49ers. When asked about the incident after the game, Singletary went on a rant about his team's lack of effort and poor attitude, culminating in the now infamous line, "It is more about them than it is about the team. Cannot play with them, cannot win with them, cannot coach with them. Can't do it. I want winners. I want people that want to win."

9. Olin Kreutz was trying hard to retire with the Bears, but he could not come to terms with the team in 2011 on a contract that would allow him to end his career in Chicago. The Bears offered him a one-year, $4 million deal that would be a significant pay cut for the six-time Pro Bowler. Despite being willing to compromise on the terms of the deal, talks broke off and the Bears signed a new center. Kreutz ended up signing a one-year contract in New Orleans, but he retired after six games due to tension in the locker room.

10. The Bears' offensive line was one of the most feared units of the early days of the NFL. Chicago had six linemen as part of the All-Decades Team for the 1920s, 1930s, and 1940s, but have had just two offensive linemen since then. Jimbo Covert was named a tackle on the 1980s team, and Olin Kreutz was the center on the 2000s squad. The Bears had seven members of their front seven on those all-decade lists, including Dick Butkus appearing on both the 1960s and 1970s teams.

CHAPTER 7:

NO AIR ZONE

QUIZ TIME!

1. How many interceptions did the Bears return for touchdowns in their famous 73-0 win over Washington in the 1940 NFL championship game?

   a. 4

   b. 3

   c. 2

   d. 1

2. Which Hall-of-Famer still holds the record for best career punt-return average and returned a kickoff 93 yards in his first career game?

   a. John "Paddy" Driscoll

   b. George McAfee

   c. Red Grange

   d. Gary Fencik

3. The top three in career interceptions in Bears history are each separated by a single interception.

a. True

b. False

4. Which Bears rookie holds the single-season record for interceptions?

a. Nathan Vasher

b. Tim Jennings

c. Mark Carrier

d. Johnny Lujack

5. Which of these players does NOT share the Bears' record with three interceptions in one game?

a. Mark Carrier

b. Richie Petitbon

c. Curtis Gentry

d. Charles Tillman

6. Brett Favre played many years in the same division as the Bears, and no team gave him more trouble than Chicago. How many times did Chicago intercept Favre in his career, more than any other team he faced?

a. 42

b. 44

c. 46

d. 48

7. Gary Fencik owns the Chicago record for most interceptions in a career, but what was his career high for interceptions in a season?

a. 4

b. 5

c. 6

d. 7

8. The Bears' record for most interceptions in a game is more than the record for fewest interceptions in a season.

    a. True

    b. False

9. Who shares the franchise record for most takeaways in a season?

    a. Gary Fencik and Charles Tillman

    b. Tim Jennings and Mike Singletary

    c. Dick Butkus and Richie Petitbon

    d. Mark Carrier and Roosevelt Taylor

10. Which team completed just one pass against the Bears in 2005, the fewest amount of completions Chicago has allowed in the modern era?

    a. Carolina Panthers

    b. Detroit Lions

    c. San Francisco 49ers

    d. Arizona Cardinals

11. What was the nickname of the Bears' safety duo of Gary Fencik and Doug Plank?

    a. The Hitmen

    b. The Maniacs

    c. The Boom Boys

    d. Rock and Hard Place

12. Which team originally drafted Gary Fencik in 1976?

    a. Dallas Cowboys
    b. New England Patriots
    c. Atlanta Falcons
    d. Miami Dolphins

13. Gary Fencik played his final season with a different team after Chicago elected not to re-sign him in 1987.

    a. True
    b. False

14. Which Bears defensive back NEVER led the league in interceptions?

    a. Tim Jennings
    b. Roosevelt Taylor
    c. Nathan Vasher
    d. Mark Carrier

15. Which linebacker holds the Bears' record for most interceptions by a non-defensive back?

    a. Doug Buffone
    b. William Perry
    c. Dick Butkus
    d. Brian Urlacher

16. How long was Nathan Vasher's return touchdown on a missed field goal in 2005 when he set the NFL record for longest play?

    a. 109 yards
    b. 108 yards

c. 107 yards

d. 106 yards

17. In which season was Charles Tillman named a First Team All-Pro after forcing 10 fumbles and returning all three of his interceptions for touchdowns?

a. 2009

b. 2010

c. 2011

d. 2012

18. How many times did Charles Tillman return an interception for a touchdown?

a. 5

b. 6

c. 7

d. 8

19. How many forced fumbles was Charles Tillman credited with during his Bears career?

a. 37

b. 40

c. 42

d. 46

20. The Bears have an interception return of more than 100 yards in their franchise's history

a. True

b. False

QUIZ ANSWERS

1. B – 3

2. B – George McAfee

3. A – True

4. C – Mark Carrier

5. D – Charles Tillman

6. A – 42

7. C – 6

8. B – False

9. D – Mark Carrier and Roosevelt Taylor

10. C – San Francisco 49ers

11. A – The Hitmen

12. D – Miami Dolphins

13. B – False

14. C – Nathan Vasher

15. A – Doug Buffone

16. B – 108 yards

17. D – 2012

18. D – 8

19. C – 42

20. A – True

DID YOU KNOW?

1. George McAfee was a two-way threat for the Bears during his brief eight-year career, which was interrupted by World War II. He was nicknamed "One-Play McAfee" for his ability to score in a variety of ways from anywhere on the field. When he set the NFL record at the time, with 12 touchdowns in 1941, the list included scores from rushing, receiving, kickoff return, punt return, interception return, and fumble return. It didn't include the fact he threw a touchdown that season as well. He was such a gamebreaker that George Halas once said he restricted McAfee's playing time in order to not ruin the league that was still in its early stages.

2. Richie Petitbon passed over football scholarships from LSU and Tulane to instead run track at Loyola University in New Orleans and study dentistry. However, the coaches at Loyola wanted Petitbon to run the 400-meter dash, and instead of converting from a sprinter, he switched schools and sports. He played quarterback for two seasons at Tulane and also held numerous kickoff return records when he left the school. Petitbon was named to the All-SEC team in 1958 before the Bears drafted him in 1959 and converted him to safety.

3. Gary Fencik was not drafted by the Bears, even though he did play his entire career for Chicago. The Miami

Dolphins originally drafted Fencik in the 10th round of the 1976 Draft out of Yale, but his career in South Florida was unfortunately cut very short. Fencik ruptured his left lung while making a tackle in a preseason game with the Saints, and he could not make it back on the field in time to make an impression on the coaching staff. He was cut by the Dolphins, but the Bears signed him during that first week of the season. Fencik, though, said he was grateful that the Dolphins thought he was good enough to play defensive back after he played wide receiver his entire career at Yale.

4. Doug Plank is the namesake—or maybe, more accurately, numbersake—of Buddy Ryan's famous 46 defense. Ryan designed the defense around Plank's hard-hitting tendencies to help a weak Chicago defense become one of the best to ever play in the NFL. Plank was a particularly ferocious tackler who was dealt more concussions than he can remember, and always loaded up on aspirin before games and kept smelling salts nearby to keep him conscious. He eventually was an assistant coach in New York with the Jets under Rex Ryan, Buddy's son, helping to pass along the 46 defense to a new generation.

5. Mark Carrier picked up the nickname "Hammer" as a rookie for a very bad reason. He kept hitting Ron Rivera in the back while going after piles, and it frustrated Rivera so much that he started calling Carrier "Hammer" for his aggressiveness and his initials. "He was not afraid of hitting anybody, even his own teammates," Rivera

told *The Athletic* in 2020. "And I thought, 'Damn, we must all look like a bunch of nails to him.' So, I called him Hammer. It made sense because his initials are M.C., just like MC Hammer." Carrier was known for being a ferocious tackler as well with 971 tackles in his first 10 seasons in the league.

6. Mike Brown's 2001 season was quite odd, but it ended with him being named a First Team All-Pro at safety despite not being a Pro Bowler. He is probably most remembered that season for the two interceptions he returned for touchdowns in overtime on consecutive weeks to propel the Bears to a 6-1 mark. On October 28, 2001, Brown ended the shortest overtime game in NFL history by intercepting Jeff Garcia on the first play of overtime and racing the other way 33 yards for the winning score. The next week, the Bears punted on their first possession of the extra session before Brown intercepted Tim Couch and returned it 16 yards for the winning touchdown to beat Cleveland.

7. It took a while for Charles Tillman to embrace his nickname "Peanut," which his aunt Rene gave him as a child. Without his signature dreadlocks, Tillman said kids used to make fun of the shape of his head, and it didn't help that his mother called him Peanut at home. It wasn't until the girls in high school thought the nickname was cute that he embraced it full-time. When he got to the NFL, Mike Brown was handing out nicknames to his new teammates and told Tillman to write his nickname on the

board or Brown would give him one. The name stuck in the Bears' locker room and quickly followed him into the media.

8. Tillman graduated from the University of Louisiana-Lafayette with a degree in criminal justice, and he is now putting that to good use in his post-football career. Tillman joined the FBI as an agent in 2018 after graduating from the training academy, though he has never confirmed it himself. Service to the United States runs in the family for Tillman, whose father, Donald Tillman Jr., was an army sergeant.

9. When the ball got into Eddie Jackson's hands during his first two years in the league, there was serious danger of the safety scoring a touchdown no matter where he was on the field. Jackson tied an NFL record with five defensive touchdowns in his first two years in the league—2017 and 2018—with three pick-sixes and two fumble returns for scores. He also joined Deion Sanders as the only two players since 1970 to have three defensive touchdowns of 65-plus yards in a two-season span. He had 12 total takeaways in his first two years, blossoming into one of the better young safeties with six interceptions in 2018.

10. Kyle Fuller comes from a football family with three brothers who played in the league at some point. His oldest brother, Vincent, played safety for six seasons with the Tennessee Titans and one with the Detroit Lions

from 2005 to 2011. Corey played two seasons for the Lions as a wide receiver. Kyle is third of the four brothers, and youngest brother, Kendall, is in his fifth season in the league having played two seasons for Washington, two for Kansas City, then re-signed in Washington before the 2020 season.

CHAPTER 8:

SUPER BOWL SALUTE

QUIZ TIME!

1. What was the final score of Super Bowl XX against the New England Patriots?

    a. 42-7

    b. 46-10

    c. 49-10

    d. 55-13

2. Where was Super Bowl XX played?

    a. New Orleans

    b. Atlanta

    c. Miami

    d. Pasadena

3. The New England Patriots never led in Super Bowl XX.

    a. True

    b. False

4. Which of these players did NOT score a touchdown for the Bears in their Super Bowl XX victory?

    a. Reggie Phillips
    b. Matt Suhey
    c. Walter Payton
    d. Jim McMahon

5. Who sacked Steve Grogan in the end zone for the safety that provided the exclamation point on the Bears' victory?

    a. Henry Waechter
    b. Richard Dent
    c. Dave Duerson
    d. Steve McMichael

6. The Bears set a record for fewest rushing yards allowed in a Super Bowl by limiting the Patriots to how many rushing yards?

    a. 19
    b. 15
    c. 12
    d. 7

7. How long was the longest field goal Kevin Butler made among the three he kicked in Super Bowl XX?

    a. 24 yards
    b. 26 yards
    c. 28 yards
    d. 30 yards

8. The Patriots' 123 yards they had against the Bears were the fewest yards ever in a Super Bowl.

    a. True
    b. False

9. Richard Dent was named the Super Bowl MVP for his performance in Super Bowl XX, but which Bears linebacker actually had more sacks in the game than Dent?

    a. Mike Singletary
    b. Wilber Marshall
    c. Jim Morrissey
    d. Otis Wilson

10. How many total yards did the Patriots lose on the Bears' record-tying seven sacks?

    a. 61
    b. 66
    c. 72
    d. 79

11. How many points did the Bears allow to the New York Giants and Los Angeles Rams on their way to winning Super Bowl XX?

    a. 0
    b. 7
    c. 10
    d. 17

12. Everyone knows the Miami Dolphins handed the Bears their only loss in 1985, but who came the next closest to beating the Bears by only losing by six points?

a. Indianapolis Colts

b. Green Bay Packers

c. Dallas Cowboys

d. Minnesota Vikings

13. Who led the Bears with seven touchdown catches during the 1985 season, but did not catch a pass in Super Bowl XX?

a. Emery Moorehead

b. Willie Gault

c. Dennis McKinnon

d. Walter Payton

14. In which defensive category did the Bears NOT lead the league in 1985?

a. Points allowed

b. Total yards allowed

c. Rushing yards allowed

d. Passing yards allowed

15. The 1985 Bears set the NFL record for most sacks in a season.

a. True

b. False

16. How long was Devin Hester's kickoff return touchdown on the opening kickoff of Super Bowl XLI?

a. 101 yards

b. 97 yards

c. 92 yards

d. 89 yards

17. Who caught the Bears' only offensive touchdown of Super Bowl XLI to give Chicago a 14-6 lead at the end of the first quarter?

   a. Thomas Jones
   b. Desmond Clark
   c. Muhsin Muhammed
   d. Bernard Berrian

18. Rex Grossman completed more than 70% of his passes in Super Bowl XLI.

   a. True
   b. False

19. Who intercepted Peyton Manning on Indianapolis' first drive of the game?

   a. Charles Tillman
   b. Chris Harris
   c. Nathan Vasher
   d. Danieal Manning

20. How many turnovers did the Bears have in their loss to the Colts in Super Bowl XLI?

   a. 2
   b. 3
   c. 4
   d. 5

QUIZ ANSWERS

1. B – 46-10

2. A – New Orleans

3. B – False

4. C – Walter Payton

5. A – Henry Waechter

6. D – 7

7. C – 28 yards

8. B – False

9. D – Otis Wilson

10. A – 61

11. A – 0

12. B – Green Bay Packers

13. C – Dennis McKinnon

14. D – Passing yards allowed

15. B – False

16. C – 92 yards

17. C – Muhsin Muhammed

18. A – True

19. B – Chris Harris

20. D – 5

DID YOU KNOW?

1. One of the most memorable parts of the Bears' run to the Super Bowl in 1985 was the hit song, "Super Bowl Shuffle." The famous music video was filmed one day after Chicago's only loss of the season and became an instant hit for the team. The song climbed as high as number 41 on Billboard charts as it sold more than half a million singles and a million videos with most of the money going to charity. It even was nominated for a Grammy for best rhythm and blues performance by a duo or group, but it lost out to "Kiss" by Prince and the Revolution. The surviving members of the team came together to do an ad for Boost Mobile ahead of Super Bowl XLIV in 2010.

2. The 1985 Bears' ferocious top-ranked defense produced four different future NFL head coaches from its ranks. Defensive back Jeff Fisher was the first to become a head coach after taking over the Houston Oilers at the end of the 1994 season. He spent 17 years with the franchise and led them to the Super Bowl in 1999. He also coached the Rams for nearly five seasons, but was fired 13 games into the 2016 season. It wasn't until 2008 when Mike Singletary became the interim coach in San Francisco that another member of the '85 Bears became a head coach. However, Singletary's stint didn't last very long as he was fired at the end of his second full season on the job. Leslie Frazier took over as the Minnesota Vikings'

coach midway through the 2010 season and kept the job for three full seasons before being fired in 2013.

3. The fourth head coach was Ron Rivera, who is the only one who bridges both of the Bears' Super Bowl appearances. Rivera played in Super Bowl XX and was Chicago's defensive coordinator in Super Bowl XLI. He became a head coach in 2011 with the Carolina Panthers and led them on one of the most successful eras in franchise history for almost nine full seasons. He coached the Panthers to the Super Bowl in 2015 when he was again foiled by a Peyton Manning-led team. After being fired in 2019 by Carolina, he became the new coach in Washington for the 2020 season.

4. Head coach Mike Ditka and defensive coordinator Buddy Ryan famously did not have a great working relationship during the 1985 season. Ryan was retained as the Bears' defensive coordinator when Chicago hired Ditka in 1982 after the players asked George Halas to keep Ryan on the staff. Ditka was known to blow up on Ryan in practice when the defense was getting the better of the offense and making it difficult for the offense to work on plays. However, Ditka said the two knew they needed each other to have success that season. "We had a helluva run," Ditka said in 2016. "Buddy had a helluva run. Was it always as smooth as it might have been? Noooo. But I don't think Buddy would've wanted it any other way. We accomplished so much together and we were never as good separately as we were together."

5. The only blemish of that 1985 season came in the most-watched *Monday Night Football* game in the program's history on December 2, 1985. Jim McMahon did not start against the Dolphins due to a sprained ankle, leaving backup Steve Fuller as the starter for the game. The game was also in Miami, so the Bears had to adjust to the humidity of a Miami evening as opposed to the cold that awaited them back in Chicago. It also didn't help that Ditka and Ryan had a public falling out after halftime after Ditka asked Ryan to make some defensive adjustments to contain Dan Marino and the Miami offense. The Bears actually outgained the Dolphins by eight yards in the game, but Marino threw three touchdown passes, and the Bears had four turnovers to seal the game.

6. William Perry's fingers are so large that there is no official size for the championship ring he was awarded after Super Bowl XX. It is believed that the ring size of 25 is the largest championship ring ever produced. It is a 10-karat gold ring with plenty of diamonds that form Chicago's trademark "C" logo on it. Perry, of course, became a cult phenomenon in the 1980s for his athletic feats despite being more than 300 pounds. He is probably most well-known for the one-yard touchdown he scored in Super Bowl XX against the Patriots.

7. The Challenger shuttle disaster occurred just two days after the Bears' Super Bowl victory, so the team was unable to visit the White House to celebrate as champions at that time. Yet 25 years later, most of the

team was able to visit Washington D.C. and visit the White House to celebrate with President Barack Obama. Among the members of the team who made the trip were coach Mike Ditka, defensive coordinator Buddy Ryan, Super Bowl MVP Richard Dent, receiver Willie Gault, and quarterback Jim McMahon. Ditka presented Obama with a number 85 Bears jersey for the occasion instead of the traditional number 1 jersey presented to the president.

8. On the 30th anniversary of the team's Super Bowl XX victory, ESPN premiered its *30 for 30* documentary on the team. The film begins with a pair of letters that help lay the foundation for the 1985 champions, one from Ditka to George Halas and the second from the Bears players to Halas to keep Ryan as the defensive coordinator. It explores the quirky personalities of the players on the team and how they all bonded through an extraordinary season.

9. The Colts' game plan heading into Super Bowl XLI was to try to keep the ball away from Devin Hester on every return opportunity. However, as the game creeped closer, Indianapolis had second thoughts about trying to avoid the Bears' return ace. The morning of the Super Bowl, Chicago's special teams coordinator showed Hester an article in the paper about Dungy's no-fear attitude on the kickoffs, which Hester admitted lit a fire under him. The Bears won the coin toss and elected to receive, and the call was a simple middle return play for

Hester. He's nearly tackled at the Chicago 20-yard line by Marlin Jackson, but a little freeze was enough for him to break free. Looking back on that moment, Hester admitted, "When I watch that move, that's a move I never did before. I guess it just came out naturally. It was an instinct."

10. Super Bowl XLI featured a pair of firsts for the NFL. The game was the first—and thus far only—Super Bowl ever played in the rain. More importantly, though, it featured the first two black head coaches in Super Bowl history as Chicago's Lovie Smith faced off against Indianapolis' Tony Dungy. The two share a bond that predated this matchup by a decade as Smith was an assistant under Dungy in Tampa Bay when Dungy was the head coach of the Buccaneers.

CHAPTER 9:

SHINING THE BUSTS

QUIZ TIME!

1. How many Hall-of-Famers have some connection to the Chicago Bears franchise?

    a. 30
    b. 33
    c. 35
    d. 38

2. How many former Bears players have been inducted into the Hall of Fame in the twenty-first century?

    a. 3
    b. 4
    c. 5
    d. 6

3. Who was NOT part of the inaugural 1963 class to be inducted into the Hall of Fame?

    a. Sid Luckman
    b. George Halas

c. Bronko Nagurski

d. Red Grange

4. The Bears had more Hall-of-Famers inducted in the 1960s than they have had since 1970.

   a. True

   b. False

5. Which Hall of Fame player did NOT win four championships with Chicago during his career?

   a. Clyde "Bulldog" Turner

   b. George McAfee

   c. Sid Luckman

   d. George Musso

6. How many players and coaches from the 1985 Bears are enshrined in the Hall of Fame?

   a. 3

   b. 4

   c. 5

   d. 6

7. Which position group features the most Bears Hall-of-Famers?

   a. Offensive line

   b. Linebackers

   c. Running backs

   d. Defensive line

8. Chicago's first-ever draft pick ended up being inducted into the Hall of Fame.

a. True

b. False

9. George Halas was presented for induction into the Hall of Fame by David L. Lawrence, who was the governor of which state?

a. Michigan

b. Pennsylvania

c. Ohio

d. Illinois

10. Who was the Bears executive inducted into the Hall of Fame in 1995 as a contributor after helping craft the Bears for nine years in the late 1970s and early 1980s?

a. Jerry Vainisi

b. Virginia McCaskey

c. Jim Finks

d. Bill Veeck

11. Which Bears Hall-of-Famer declined to wear a helmet until 1943 when the NFL required a helmet for all players?

a. Bill Hewitt

b. Dan Fortmann

c. Bronko Nagurski

d. Link Lyman

12. Joe Stydahar sent a message by wearing which number during his Hall of Fame career?

a. 1

b. 6

c. 10

d. 13

13. How old was Gale Sayers when he became the youngest inductee into the Pro Football Hall of Fame?

   a. 41

   b. 37

   c. 36

   d. 34

14. George Trafton interrupted his professional football career to spend a year as an assistant coach at Northwestern.

   a. True

   b. False

15. How many NFL records did Walter Payton hold when he retired from the NFL?

   a. 14

   b. 16

   c. 18

   d. 21

16. After only recording three sacks as a rookie, Richard Dent had double-digit sacks in eight of his final 10 years in Chicago during his first tenure. Which years did he NOT reach 10 sacks?

   a. 1988 and 1992

   b. 1986 and 1991

   c. 1989 and 1992

   d. 1987 and 1990

17. How many takeaways did Dick Butkus have as a rookie with the Bears?

    a. 15
    b. 11
    c. 8
    d. 3

18. Brian Urlacher was elected to the Hall of Fame in his first year of eligibility.

    a. True
    b. False

19. Jimbo Covert and Ed Sprinkle were both set to be inducted in 2020. When was the last time the Bears had two people inducted in the same year?

    a. 1965
    b. 1974
    c. 1982
    d. 1993

20. What was the first year a member of the Bears franchise was NOT elected to the Hall of Fame?

    a. 1965
    b. 1966
    c. 1967
    d. 1968

QUIZ ANSWERS

1. C – 35

2. D – 6

3. A – Sid Luckman

4. B – False

5. B – George McAfee

6. D – 6

7. A – Offensive line

8. A – True

9. B – Pennsylvania

10. C – Jim Finks

11. A – Bill Hewitt

12. D – 13

13. D – 34

14. A – True

15. B – 16

16. C – 1989 and 1992

17. B – 11

18. A – True

19. C – 1982

20. D – 1968

DID YOU KNOW?

1. Clyde Turner actually gave himself the nickname "Bulldog" when he enrolled at Hardin-Simmons to play college football. He was on the team with his best friend, A.J. Roy, who Turner nicknamed "Tiger," and the two would use these names to refer to each other on the practice field. The name stuck with Turner throughout his tenure in Chicago, where he played both sides of the ball and multiple positions on both sides. He was mostly a lineman on offense, but he did have a 48-yard touchdown run when he was given carries in emergency situations. Turner semi-regretted his nickname as he got older, lamenting, "It's a little embarrassing to be called Bulldog when you're over 50, but I guess it beats the hell out of Clyde."

2. Link Lyman did not play any high school football growing up in McDonald, Kansas, because there were only six or seven boys in the entire school. That didn't stop him from playing for three years at Nebraska before jumping into the professional game in 1922. He played seven seasons for the Bears over a nine-year period, taking off the 1929 season to play semi-pro football, then focusing on other business ventures in 1932. George Halas believed Lyman was stronger in 1933 and 1934, his final two seasons with the Bears, than he was when Lyman originally joined the team in 1925.

3. George Trafton was a tough man to play against, and legend has it he forced four players out of a 1920 game against Rock Island as the center for the Decatur Staleys. Red Grange called him "the toughest, meanest, most ornery critter alive" as Chicago's starting center for 13 seasons. Trafton joined the Bears because he was kicked off Notre Dame's team for playing with semi-professional teams under aliases for some extra money. He is credited as the first center to snap the ball with one hand, a product of his missing index finger on his left hand. He also participated in five boxing matches to help survive the Great Depression, winning the first four before being knocked out by heavyweight champion Primo Carnera in his final bout.

4. George Blanda probably was not destined for the Hall of Fame during 10 seasons with the Bears after Chicago drafted him in the 12th round of the 1949 NFL Draft. He was not the full-time starting quarterback for the Bears until 1953, his fifth season in the league, then he was beset by injuries the following year, and he lost the starting job. The Bears wanted to make him a kicker in 1959, but Blanda was upset by the proposal and retired instead. In 1960, the American Football League came calling, and Blanda started the second half of his career that ultimately earned him a spot in Canton.

5. Stan Jones was a workout pioneer for the NFL, which turned him into a ferocious beast on the field for the Bears. He started his career in 1954 as an offensive tackle

for Chicago, but switched to guard the following year, where he spent the next eight seasons. He played both sides of the ball in 1962 and moved over to defensive tackle permanently in 1963. Jones played 12 years for the Bears, but he was traded to Washington in 1965 as a favor from George Halas to Jones, so Jones could play near his home in Rockville, Maryland.

6. Mike Ditka revolutionized what it meant to be a tight end in the NFL when he entered the league in 1961. The position was mostly known as being a blocker, but Ditka combined excellent blocking with tremendous catching, and he became an active receiver in the offense. He set the record for most receptions by a tight end in 1964, which held up until 1980 when the 16-game season had already been introduced. He didn't miss a single start for the Bears, starting all 84 games from his rookie season until he left the team in 1967. Ditka was the first tight end elected to the Hall of Fame when he was inducted in 1988.

7. Alan Page played just three and a half seasons for the Bears at the end of his career after the Vikings waived him in the middle of the 1978 season. Page was immediately embraced in Chicago and helped improve the struggling unit, and he was rewarded with a new contract that paid him more than he made in Minnesota. When he joined the Bears, he was already an attorney in Minnesota, a job that would play a large role in his post-football life. He was elected to the Minnesota Supreme Court in 1992 as the first black justice on the court, then

was re-elected in 1998 as the biggest vote-getter in Minnesota history. He easily won re-election in 2004 and 2010 before being forced to step down in August 2015 when he reached the mandatory retirement age of 70.

8. Doug Atkins arrived in Knoxville, Tennessee, on a basketball scholarship to the University of Tennessee. However, Robert R. Neyland, the Volunteers' football coach, saw Atkins's size and agility and recruited him to come play on the football team. He was an All-American in 1952, and he was an SEC champion in the high jump, a skill that helped him develop into an elite pass rusher. Atkins openly clashed with George Halas during his 12 seasons in Chicago as their personalities—Atkins a free-flowing, laid-back free spirit and Halas a fiery general—clashed, but the relationship worked well. Atkins was a key member of the Bears' 1963 championship team, and Halas said when Atkins retired in 1969 that there was no defensive end in history better than Atkins.

9. Few people outside of Chicago will remember Orlando Pace's tenure with the Bears because it didn't last very long. Pace started the first 11 games of the 2009 season for the Bears, but he lost his starting position after injuring his groin. Pace was cut by the Rams in 2009 as a salary-cap casualty, but he signed the same day the Bears acquired Jay Cutler from the Broncos. He said he signed with Chicago because he wanted a chance at another Super Bowl ring. Instead, the Bears went 7-9, and Pace was cut the following March and ended up retiring.

10. There are so many plays that can be considered Brian Urlacher's finest with the Bears. One that makes most people's list is the strip he had against the Arizona Cardinals in 2006 on *Monday Night Football*. Bears coach Lovie Smith recalled trying to pump up Urlacher between the third and fourth quarters, telling him, "You're freaking Brian Urlacher. You need to make something happen right now." He did make something happen, with about five minutes left in the game, when he punched the ball out of Edgerrin James's hands and Charles Tillman scooped up the ball and returned it for a touchdown that brought the Bears within six points. Urlacher had 19 tackles in that game—25 after review from the Bears coaching staff—and the Hall-of-Famer himself called it one of his best games in his career.

CHAPTER 10:

DRAFT DAY

QUIZ TIME!

1. The first draft pick in Bears history was Joe Stydahar out of West Virginia. Which pick did the Bears use to select him?

   a. 6th
   b. 8th
   c. 12th
   d. 14th

2. Later in that 1936 NFL Draft, the Bears selected a second Hall-of-Famer. Who was Chicago's 9th round selection in that draft?

   a. George Musso
   b. George McAfee
   c. Bill Hewitt
   d. Danny Fortmann

3. The Chicago Bears have drafted 1st overall since the AFL-NFL merger in 1970.

a. True

b. False

4. Which school has produced the most Chicago Bears draft picks?

   a. Ohio State

   b. Northwestern

   c. Notre Dame

   d. USC

5. Which of these future Hall-of-Famers was NOT a 1st round selection by the Bears?

   a. George McAfee

   b. Sid Luckman

   c. Clyde "Bulldog" Turner

   d. Bobby Layne

6. The Bears have made many notable draft picks inside the top five, who was NOT one of those selections?

   a. Mark Carrier

   b. Jim McMahon

   c. Mike Ditka

   d. Dick Butkus

7. Bill George was one of the Bears' three 1st round selections in the 1951 Draft.

   a. True

   b. False

8. In which round did the Bears draft receiver Harlon Hill out of North Alabama in 1954?

a. 7th

b. 10th

c. 12th

d. 15th

9. The 1965 NFL Draft was famous for the Bears drafting Dick Butkus and Gale Sayers with consecutive selections in the 1st round. However, the Bears had a third 1st round pick in that draft. Who did Chicago select with that pick?

    a. Dick Evey

    b. Jim Nance

    c. Steve DeLong

    d. Billy Martin

10. Walter Payton was drafted with which pick in the 1975 NFL Draft?

    a. 2nd

    b. 3rd

    c. 4th

    d. 5th

11. The 1983 NFL Draft is arguably the best one the Bears have ever had because they drafted several stars of the 1985 Super Bowl champions. Who was NOT part of this iconic draft class?

    a. Richard Dent

    b. Willie Gault

    c. Dave Duerson

    d. Wilber Marshall

12. In which round of the 1985 Draft did the Bears select Kevin Butler, who kicked three field goals in Super Bowl XX?

    a. 2nd
    b. 4th
    c. 6th
    d. 8th

13. Jim Harbaugh completed more passes as a member of the Bears than any other quarterback Chicago has ever drafted.

    a. True
    b. False

14. Which mainstay of the Bears offensive line did Chicago find in the 3rd round of the 1998 NFL Draft?

    a. James Williams
    b. Chris Villarrial
    c. John Tait
    d. Olin Kreutz

15. Which pick did the Bears have in the 2000 NFL Draft when they selected Brian Urlacher in the 1st round?

    a. 7th
    b. 9th
    c. 11th
    d. 12th

16. Who did the Bears draft in the 7th round of the 2010 NFL Supplementary Draft that cost them their 7th round selection in the 2011 Draft?

a. J.T. Thomas

b. Isaiah Frey

c. J'Marcus Webb

d. Harvey Unga

17. Who was the Bears' 1st round pick in 2003 before they traded back into the 1st round to draft Rex Grossman?

a. Michael Haynes

b. Tommie Harris

c. Marc Colombo

d. Greg Olsen

18. Which of these 1st round busts had the shortest tenure in Chicago with the Bears?

a. Cedric Benson

b. Kevin White

c. Cade McNown

d. Curtis Enis

19. Prior to 2019-20, the Bears had never gone consecutive years without drafting in the 1st round.

a. True

b. False

20. Which position have the Bears drafted most in the 1st round?

a. Defensive end

b. Offensive tackle

c. Running back

d. Offensive guard

QUIZ ANSWERS

1. A – 6th

2. D – Danny Fortmann

3. B – False

4. C – Notre Dame

5. A – George McAfee

6. A – Mark Carrier

7. B – False

8. D – 15th

9. C – Steve DeLong

10. C – 4th

11. D – Wilber Marshall

12. B – 4th

13. A – True

14. D – Olin Kreutz

15. B – 9th

16. D – Harvey Unga

17. A – Michael Haynes

18. C – Cade McNown

19. B – False

20. C – Running back

DID YOU KNOW?

1. Over the course of the Bears' history, they have drafted their fair share of busts in addition to success stories. They have also drafted several players who made a name for themselves in capacities outside of playing for the Bears. Chicago drafted Don Meredith in the 3rd round of the 1960 NFL Draft, but he chose to sign with the Cowboys in the American Football League instead. In 1972, the Bears drafted quarterback Jim Fassel, who was the Giants' head coach from 1997-2003 and a longtime assistant in the league.

2. The scouting process for the first NFL Draft in 1936 was far different than what it is today. Few teams actually went out to scout college players and instead relied upon national reporting to influence their picks. George Halas didn't leave his first pick up to chance and ended up taking the advice of one of his own players, Bill Karr. The Bears' end had played with Joe Stydahar at West Virginia and vouched for the tackle's skills, so Chicago surprised many by then selecting "Jumbo Joe" with its first pick in the draft. Unlike so many of the busts from that draft, Stydahar became a Hall-of-Famer as an anchor of Chicago's formidable offensive line.

3. One of the most fortunate trades in Bears history came on December 2, 1963, more than a year before the two teams

involved knew the implications of the deal. Chicago dealt the 28th pick in the 1964 Draft along with the 51st pick in the 1964 Draft to Pittsburgh for the Steelers' 1st round pick in the 1965 NFL Draft. The Steelers would draft tight end Jim Kelly with the 28th pick and defensive end Ben McGee at number 51, and only McGee had a grand impact on Pittsburgh's fortunes. However, that 1st round pick in 1965 became the 3rd overall pick in the draft. The Bears owned the 4th pick from their own misfortunes in the 1964 season and ended up altering the course of their franchise with those two picks. Chicago used the Pittsburgh pick to draft Dick Butkus, then followed up by drafting Gale Sayers with their own 1st round selection.

4. Ted Albrecht's promising career was ended by a back injury that forced him to miss the 1982 season. He started 75 of the 77 games he played in after being a 1st round pick in 1977, but he realized his career was over during training camp in 1983 when he was trying to return from two ruptured discs in his back. He was an All-Rookie team member in 1977 as Chicago made the playoffs, and he was part of the offensive line that helped Walter Payton set the single-game rushing record that season. After purchasing and expanding his own travel agency in his retirement, Albrecht rejoined the football scene as a color analyst for Northwestern football, a position he still holds for the 2020 season.

5. Mike Singletary was frustrated on draft day 1981 when three teams told him they were going to potentially draft

him before deciding on the other guy. When he wasn't drafted in the 1st round, he said he had the usual young, immature doubts of his abilities. But in that moment of prayer, he said he prayed, "You know what Lord, I don't know if I'm going to play this game, but if you really want me to play, please let me get drafted by the Chicago Bears." About a minute later, the Bears traded up to select Singletary in the 2nd round with the 38th overall pick.

6. The Bears' famous 1983 Draft featured plenty of interesting stories about how Chicago drafted seven starters for their 1985 Super Bowl championship team. There was Hall of Fame tackle Jimbo Covert, who couldn't watch the draft so he didn't know Chicago drafted him until three picks later. His brothers were tying up the phone lines by inviting people to the draft party, but it prevented Covert's agent from calling him with the good news. Then, there was Richard Dent, who had been given a 2nd round grade by Bears scouts, but Chicago was helpless in watching the 5th, 6th, and 7th rounds of the draft that year after trading away its picks. The Bears assumed Dent would be gone by the time their 8th round pick arrived, but instead, Dent was there and became a cornerstone of Chicago's defense.

7. The Cade McNown tenure in Chicago was a disaster throughout his two seasons with the Bears. He angered teammates by passing the blame for his own mistakes. He upset them with a terrible week of practice and

preparation for a 2000 game against the 49ers, forcing the offense to apologize to the defense for what was about to come that Sunday. McNown was also ill-prepared for the NFL game; something coach Dick Jauron admitted in 2001 when the Bears were set to trade or release the quarterback. "I had and have confidence in Cade's ability, but I certainly overestimated where he was and then where he would go."

8. The Bears were split on which cornerback to take with the 57th pick in the 2006 NFL Draft. Chicago was waiting for Baltimore to make its pick at number 56 and discussing whether to select Devin Hester or Ashton Youboty with their turn. The room was still split when then-general manager Jerry Angelo asks each of the primary scouts to go over their reports one last time. Mark Sadowski, currently the Bears' director of college scouting, makes the case for Hester by explaining that Hester is the fastest player he's seen with the ball in his hands even though he isn't the more polished defensive back. Ten months later, the Bears are in Miami for Super Bowl XLI, and Hester is back in the city where he became a college star and returning the opening kickoff for a touchdown.

9. Former Bears general manager Jerry Angelo, like many people, was skeptical about players who put up prolific numbers in the non-power conferences. That was the case with Matt Forte entering the 2008 Senior Bowl, where he ended up being the MVP of the game. The Bears kept a closer eye on Forte through the individual

drills and game, and Angelo said he came away impressed with Forte's professionalism and attitude. No one, though, might have been as impressed as then-Bears scout Chris Ballard, who continued to campaign for the Bears to draft Forte. Now the general manager of the Colts, Ballard was very passionate about Forte to the point where Angelo joked that they drafted Forte just to shut up Ballard.

10. Chicago's 2020 2nd round pick Cole Kmet has a deep connection to the Bears franchise. His dad, Frank, was a defensive lineman on the team's practice squad in 1993, and Kmet grew up rooting for the Bears in suburban Chicago. The family was understandably excited when coach Matt Nagy called to congratulate Kmet on becoming the newest member of the Bears. However, Chicago's interest in Kmet was a secret as the Bears worked hard to keep their communications with the tight end secretive throughout the process. Kmet didn't even know the Bears were interested until the NFL Combine when a Bears coach quickly pulled him to the side to explain the situation. Chicago selecting Kmet 43rd overall is the highest they've drafted a player out of Notre Dame since the AFL-NFL merger in 1970.

CHAPTER 11:

LET'S MAKE A DEAL

QUIZ TIME!

1. The Bears have completed a trade with every NFL team.

    a. True

    b. False

2. Which of these players did the Bears NOT trade to Pittsburgh between 1960 and 1963?

    a. Clyde Brock

    b. Harlon Hill

    c. Rudy Bukich

    d. Art Anderson

3. Who was the running back the Bears coveted enough to send defensive back Frank Budka, center Joe Wendryhoski, and guard Roger Davis to the Rams?

    a. Ronnie Bull

    b. Joe Marconi

    c. Preston Powell

    d. Jon Arnett

4. Which AFL team tried to sign Mike Ditka in 1967 that caused the Bears to trade the tight end to the Philadelphia Eagles?

   a. Oakland Raiders
   b. Houston Oilers
   c. Kansas City Chiefs
   d. Buffalo Bills

5. Who was the quarterback the Bears acquired in the trade with the Eagles for Mike Ditka?

   a. Larry Rakestraw
   b. King Hill
   c. Jack Concannon
   d. Virgil Carter

6. Which guard did the Bears acquire from New Orleans in the trade that sent Doug Atkins and Herman Lee to the Saints?

   a. Jim Cadile
   b. George Seals
   c. Palmer Pyle
   d. Don Croftcheck

7. How many combined 1st round selections did the Bears acquire when trading Willie Gault and Wilber Marshall in the 1988 offseason?

   a. 0
   b. 2
   c. 3
   d. 4

8. The Bears received seven picks from the Eagles in exchange for the number 81 pick in the 1989 NFL Draft.

   a. True

   b. False

9. Which player did the Bears NOT send away in the trade with Dallas for linebacker Barry Minter?

   a. Jim Schwantz

   b. John Roper

   c. Markus Paul

   d. Kelly Blackwell

10. How many draft picks did Chicago acquire from Washington when trading the number 7 pick in the 1999 Draft?

    a. 4

    b. 3

    c. 6

    d. 5

11. The Bears were very active on draft day in 2000 and traded its 4th, 5th, 6th, and 7th round picks at some point that day.

    a. True

    b. False

12. The Bears originally had the number 4 pick in the 2003 NFL Draft. Which team did they trade the selection to on draft day in order to obtain two 1st round picks and a 4th round pick in the 2003 Draft?

a. New England Patriots

b. Cincinnati Bengals

c. New York Jets

d. Cleveland Browns

13. Which defensive lineman came over from Miami in the trade that sent Marty Booker to the Dolphins?

a. Alex Brown

b. Adewale Ogunleye

c. Ian Scott

d. Brendon Ayanbadejo

14. Which hard-hitting safety played his final season in Chicago after being acquired for a 6th round pick?

a. Adam Archuleta

b. Dante Wesley

c. Brandon McGowan

d. Mike Brown

15. Who did the Bears draft with the one pick they received from the Broncos in the Jay Cutler trade?

a. Dan LeFevour

b. Henry Melton

c. Joshua Moore

d. Johnny Knox

16. The Bears traded up in the 2012 NFL Draft to select Alshon Jeffery in the 2nd round.

a. True

b. False

17. Which special teams ace did Chicago trade for in 2012 when they sent Tyler Clutts to the Houston Texans?

    a. Sherrick McManis
    b. Armando Allen
    c. Blake Costanzo
    d. J.T. Thomas

18. Who did the Bears draft with the 5ᵗʰ round selection they acquired in the Brandon Marshall trade to the Jets?

    a. Brock Vereen
    b. Jonathan Bostic
    c. David Fales
    d. Adrian Amos

19. How many total draft picks did the Bears surrender to the Raiders in the Khalil Mack trade?

    a. 2
    b. 3
    c. 4
    d. 5

20. Which round was the draft pick the Bears sent to Jacksonville to acquire Nick Foles in 2020?

    a. 3rd
    b. 4th
    c. 5th
    d. 6th

QUIZ ANSWERS

1. B – False

2. A – Clyde Brock

3. D – Jon Arnett

4. B – Houston Oilers

5. C – Jack Concannon

6. D – Don Croftcheck

7. C – 3

8. A – True

9. A – Jim Schwantz

10. D – 5

11. B – False

12. C – New York Jets

13. B – Adewale Ogunleye

14. A – Adam Archuleta

15. D – Johnny Knox

16. A – True

17. A – Sherrick McManis

18. D – Adrian Amos

19. C – 4

20. B – 4th

DID YOU KNOW?

1. The Bears were the first team to trade for a draft choice, doing so in 1947 to draft Bobby Layne with the 3rd overall pick in the 1948 NFL Draft. Layne was not done with famous trades with the Bears, and Chicago traded him after one year because he was unhappy with being third on the depth chart. The Bears shipped him to the New York Bulldogs for a draft pick and some cash and was one of the first candidates inducted into the Hall of Fame in the 1960s.

2. Doug Flutie lasted less than a year in Chicago after his rights were acquired in 1986 on October 14. On October 13, 1987, the Bears shipped him off to New England so he could play for the Patriots during the strike. At the time, Flutie knew he wasn't going to play in Chicago after the strike ended so he forced his way into a better position for his career. Flutie had played in four games in 1986 for Chicago and started the team's playoff game that season, but had fallen out of favor before the trade.

3. Dick Butkus was not the only Hall-of-Famer the Bears drafted with picks they acquired the year prior. Chicago also traded for Pittsburgh's 1st round pick in 1939 prior to the 1938 season, and used that selection to draft Sid Luckman. More recently, though, three weeks before the 1978 Draft, Chicago sent Wally Chambers to Tampa Bay

for tight end Bob Moore and the Buccaneers' 1st round pick in 1979. That draft choice turned into Dan Hampton, an anchor of the Bears' defense for 12 seasons and a critical member of the 1985 Bears defense.

4. There is a debate about the worst trade in Bears history, but that discussion is rarely brought up without mentioning the Rick Mirer trade. Chicago sent its 1st round pick in 1997 to Seattle for Mirer, who never lived up to his billing as the 2nd overall pick in the 1993 NFL Draft and spent most of 1996 as a backup. The Bears were worried about their quarterback situation at the time of the trade, but Mirer started just three games while appearing in seven and threw six interceptions to zero touchdowns. Had the Bears kept the 11th pick in the draft, they could have drafted Warrick Dunn, who was the 12th pick that season, or Tony Gonzalez, who was drafted 13th.

5. The Bears decided in 2007 that it was time for them to move on from Thomas Jones, so they traded him to the New York Jets while also swapping 2nd round picks. At the time, Chicago was pinning its hope on Cedric Benson becoming the feature back for the offense, but that never materialized. Instead, the trade sent shockwaves through the locker room and created a lot of anger among the players. A year later, linebacker Lance Briggs voiced his frustrations about the Bears trading away their best offensive player, who also happened to be a very important leader on the team. After his retirement, Brian

Urlacher said the trade marked the start of the end for the Bears in the 2000s because Chicago never replaced Jones's leadership in the locker room.

6. The trade tree from the Jay Cutler trade reverberated around the entire NFL community as Denver figured out how to use the picks it acquired. The Broncos eventually traded the 113th pick, the 4th round pick the Bears surrendered, to New England, which used it to draft Aaron Hernandez. The Patriots also acquired the 24th pick in that trade with Denver and then they flipped that pick to Dallas, which ended up drafting Dez Bryant in that spot. Tim Tebow was drafted through the many trades Denver made with the picks it acquired from Chicago, and those subsequent trades also netted the Patriots Devin McCourty and gave the Steelers the pick they used to draft Mike Wallace.

7. Greg Olsen was well on his way to becoming one of the best tight ends of this era when the Bears traded him to Carolina in 2011. Olsen caught 194 passes for nearly 2,000 yards and 20 touchdowns when the Bears traded him right before training camp. At the time, Olsen was not a great fit in offensive coordinator Mike Martz's system, but he was a favorite target of Jay Cutler. In hindsight, former general manager Jerry Angelo admitted it was a bad trade because Olsen was the Bears' best receiver at the time, and he shouldn't have let him walk out the door. The only way to soften that blow is that the Bears packaged the 3rd round pick it received

from the Panthers with its own 3rd round pick to trade for Brandon Marshall, arguably the best receiver in the team's history.

8. The Bears have never made a trade with the Baltimore Ravens, but the two sides nearly had a deal during the 2011 Draft. Chicago was supposed to move up to number 26 from number 29 and send the Ravens a 4th round pick as well to complete the deal. However, the Bears never called in the trade to the league office due to a miscommunication between two staffers. The Bears drafted Wisconsin tackle Gabe Carimi at 29th overall, the same player Chicago was trying to move up to draft. NFL commissioner Roger Goodell strongly suggested the Bears relinquish a draft pick as compensation for the mix-up, but the Bears declined to do so.

9. One of the most talked about trades in recent years for the Bears was the decision in 2017 to move up one spot to 2nd overall to draft Mitchell Trubisky. The North Carolina quarterback was reportedly a hot commodity for teams as they tried to trade with the San Francisco 49ers for the pick. The Bears ended up surrendering the 3rd overall pick, a 3rd round and 4th round pick in 2017, as well as a 3rd round pick in 2018. It was a trade that shocked many experts, but general manager Ryan Pace told reporters, "You always feel like there's competition. So when you have conviction on something—you never know half the time. It's like in free agency, when the agent tells you he's got three other teams he's working

with. You never really know. You've just got to trust your conviction on it, and if you want a player you aggressively go get him."

10. The trade for Khalil Mack in 2018 was one that instantly upgraded the Bears' defense with one of the game's best pass rushers now on the roster. The process to acquire him, though, was a tedious process that involved many phone calls between the general managers and many more between the coaches throughout training camp. Finally, on the final night of the preseason, with roster cut day looming, the Raiders asked every team to send in their best offer. Most of the Bears management did not watch that fourth preseason game, and the fax came in the next day that the Raiders had accepted Chicago's offer. After less than three hours talking with Mack and his representatives, a new contract was agreed to, and the Bears management slept well that night knowing the hard work was over.

CHAPTER 12:

WRITING THE RECORD BOOK

QUIZ TIME!

1. Which record did Gale Sayers NOT set during his rookie year in 1965?

    a. NFL record for touchdowns as a rookie

    b. Bears record for receiving touchdowns as a rookie

    c. Bears record for touchdowns in a season

    d. Bears record for rushing touchdowns in a season

2. Gale Sayers also set the Bears' rookie scoring record in 1965, but that was broken by which kicker, who held the NFL record until 2014?

    a. Kevin Butler

    b. Paul Edinger

    c. Robbie Gould

    d. Jeff Jaeger

3. As he continued to rewrite the Bears' record book as a rookie, Gale Sayers set the record for most points and touchdowns in a game when he scored how many times against San Francisco?

a. 24 points, 4 touchdowns

b. 32 points, 5 touchdowns

c. 36 points, 6 touchdowns

d. 42 points, 7 touchdowns

4. Who holds the Bears' record for most two-point conversions with six in his Chicago career?

a. Martellus Bennett

b. Thomas Jones

c. Matt Forte

d. Greg Olsen

5. Walter Payton has twice as many rushing touchdowns in his career as the running back with the second-most rushing touchdowns in Bears history.

a. True

b. False

6. How many times did Walter Payton run for 100 yards in a game during his career, easily the most in Bears history?

a. 66

b. 69

c. 73

d. 77

7. Who holds the Bears' record with 36 completions in a game?

a. Erik Kramer

b. Josh McCown

c. Sid Luckman

d. Jay Cutler

8. Shane Matthews set the Bears' record for most consecutive completions in a 2000 game against the Patriots. How many straight passes did he complete in the game?

   a. 18
   b. 17
   c. 16
   d. 15

9. Which of these quarterbacks did NOT have four 300-yard passing games in a season and therefore does not share the Chicago record for single-season 300-yard performances?

   a. Erik Kramer
   b. Jay Cutler
   c. Bill Wade
   d. Mitchell Trubisky

10. The Bears' rookie record for receptions is held by a wide receiver.

    a. True
    b. False

11. Who holds the Bears' record for the most career receiving touchdowns?

    a. Gale Sayers
    b. Harlon Hill
    c. Curtis Conway
    d. Ken Kavanaugh

12. Which defensive lineman holds the franchise record for most safeties in his career, with three?

a. Richard Dent

b. Steve McMichael

c. Doug Atkins

d. Israel Idonije

13. Who held the Bears' unofficial record for sacks in a season before sacks became an official statistic in 1982?

a. Doug Atkins

b. Dick Butkus

c. Jim Osbourne

d. Wally Chambers

14. How many combined return yards did Devin Hester have with the Bears to set the franchise record?

a. 8,745

b. 9,132

c. 9,328

d. 9,500

15. Robbie Gould holds the record for most extra points made in Bears history.

a. True

b. False

16. How many 50-plus-yard field goals did Robbie Gould make in his career with the Bears?

a. 17

b. 19

c. 21

d. 23

17. Which quarterback hung 509 passing yards on the Bears in 1982 to set Chicago's record for most passing yards allowed?

    a. Lynn Dickey

    b. Doug Williams

    c. Vince Ferragamo

    d. Joe Montana

18. Which divisional nemesis was responsible for the longest offensive play at Soldier Field?

    a. Aaron Rodgers

    b. Brett Favre

    c. Adrian Peterson

    d. Barry Sanders

19. Which Hall-of-Famer torched Chicago for 20 catches and 283 yards to set the Bears' records for receptions and receiving yards allowed in a game.

    a. Terrell Owens

    b. Steve Largent

    c. Cris Carter

    d. Jerry Rice

20. The Bears set an NFL record in a 1942 game with Detroit by forcing the Lions into how many turnovers?

    a. 9

    b. 10

    c. 11

    d. 12

QUIZ ANSWERS

1. B – Bears record for receiving touchdowns as a rookie

2. A – Kevin Butler

3. C – 36 points, 6 touchdowns

4. C – Matt Forte

5. A – True

6. D – 77

7. B – Josh McCown

8. D – 15

9. A – Erik Kramer

10. B – False

11. D – Ken Kavanaugh

12. B – Steve McMichael

13. C – Jim Osbourne

14. A – 8,745

15. B – False

16. D – 23

17. C – Vince Ferragamo

18. B – Brett Favre

19. A – Terrell Owens

20. D – 12

DID YOU KNOW?

1. Johnny Lujack set the Bears' record for passing in the season finale of the 1949 season, and no quarterback has touched the record since then. Lujack completed 24 of his 39 attempts for 468 yards and six touchdowns while also tossing three interceptions. The Bears handily beat the Chicago Cardinals that day, 52-21, as Ken Kavanaugh and John Hoffman both caught two touchdown passes. Bill Wade came two yards shy of the record in 1962, but otherwise, no one has come within 40 yards of the record since it was set.

2. Michael Jordan was the second Chicago athlete famous for a "Flu Game." The first was almost 20 years earlier on November 20, 1977, when Walter Payton set the NFL record with 275 rushing yards in a 10-7 win over the Vikings. Not only did Payton obliterate the old Bears record of 205 yards set by Gale Sayers and matched by Payton earlier in 1977, he did so while sick. After the game, Payton admitted to feeling queasy right up until kickoff and that he had hot and cold flashes throughout the week. His performance was memorable because he also became the third player in NFL history to rush for at least 200 yards more than once and broke his own Bears record for yards in a season.

3. Similar to Payton, Alshon Jeffery broke the Bears' record for most receiving yards in a game twice in the same

season. He did it the first time on October 6, 2013, when he caught 10 passes for 218 yards in a loss to New Orleans, which broke a nearly 60-year-old record. The new record didn't even last 60 days before Jeffery torched the Vikings for 249 yards and two scores on 12 catches, though Minnesota won the game in overtime. Jeffery ended that season with 1,421 yards, just 87 yards shy of the franchise record for most receiving yards in a season.

4. It's rare enough to see one kickoff returned for a touchdown in the NFL; it's even rarer for two from the same player in the same game. Yet on *Monday Night Football* on December 11, 2006, Devin Hester returned a pair of kickoffs back for touchdowns. Those kick returns broke the NFL record for most return touchdowns in a season as his fifth and sixth scores in his rookie campaign, if you include the missed field goal he returned for a touchdown that season. He put the Bears in the lead with a 94-yard kickoff return in the second quarter after the Rams scored a touchdown. Hester then sealed the game with a 96-yard return in the fourth quarter to end any chance at a comeback.

5. When it comes to the topic of sacks in the Bears' record book, it's safe to assume Richard Dent owns the record. He owns the career record, single-season record, and single-game record for both the regular season and postseason. He was a major part of the defense all three times the Bears had at least 10 sacks in a game and in the three seasons with the most sacks in franchise history.

6. There have been some excellent running backs in the Bears' storied history, but none of them rushed for more yards than Thomas Jones did on January 21, 2007. Jones led the way for the Bears' offense in a snowy NFC championship game to help Chicago reach the Super Bowl for the first time since 1985. He had his own personal touchdown drive where he ran the ball on all eight plays and gained 69 yards, the last two propelling him into the end zone. He later scored a 15-yard touchdown for the final points in the game. Jones then ran for 112 yards in the rain at Super Bowl XLI for the third-most rushing yards in a postseason game in Bears history.

7. Only twice since 1980 have the Bears overcome a 20-point deficit to win a game, tied for the largest comeback in franchise history. The first was in 1987 against Tampa Bay, but the second might be the most famous comeback in Bears history. Chicago entered its game on October 16, 2006, with a 5-0 record, but quickly fell behind the Arizona Cardinals 20-0. Chicago scored two defensive touchdowns, and Hester returned a punt for a score late in the fourth quarter to win the game. The Bears became the first team in NFL history to successfully rally from 20-plus points down without scoring an offensive touchdown. And the victory set up the infamous Dennis Green "they are who we thought they were" meltdown in his postgame press conference.

8. The Bears have had a 300-yard passer just 83 times in their history, and a few times, they've even come in consecutive

games. But only three quarterbacks have been able to throw for 300 yards in three straight games, and only one—Brian Hoyer in 2016—could do it in four straight games. Hoyer's streak was ended not by great defense but poor luck during the 2016 season. He took over for Jay Cutler after Cutler was hurt in a Week 2 loss to Philadelphia, then threw for 300 yards in each of his next four starts. He fell three yards shy of becoming the fifth Chicago quarterback to throw for 400 yards in a game on October 9 in a loss to the Colts. His streak ended though when he broke his arm early in the second quarter against the Green Bay Packers, which also ended his season.

9. Patrick Mannelly has played more games for the Bears than any other player in team history after spending 16 full seasons with the franchise. He was the team's long snapper from day one, after being a 6th round choice in the 1998 NFL Draft, and the Bears recorded him making 2,282 long snaps in his career. He also was excellent in punt coverage and was credited with 81 special-teams tackles, the third-most of anyone on the team at the time of his retirement. He was part of the punting unit that set NFL records for most consecutive punts without having one blocked (920) and 180 consecutive games without allowing a punt to be blocked. He missed just 11 games in his career while playing in all 16 games 12 times during his career, and in 15 on three other occasions.

10. Call it a curse, a hex, or whatever you want, but the Bears have not had consistent kicking luck since cutting

Robbie Gould before the 2016 season. Gould left Chicago as the franchise's career leader in scoring, field goals made, 50-plus-yard field goals made, and field goal percentage. What made the departure so shocking was in 2015, Gould set the Bears' record for most field goals in a season (33) and most field goals of longer than 50 yards (7) in a season. Over the next four seasons, the Bears kickers made just 77.7% of their kicks and made just six field goals longer than 50 yards. In that same span, Gould made 90.5% of his field goals with six field goals of more than 50 yards.

CONCLUSION

If we've done our job correctly, you've reached this point chock-full of new facts about your favorite NFL team, the Chicago Bears. Whether it's which notable players still hold franchise records or some of the behind-the-scenes information about how some of your favorite players arrived in Chicago, we hope you enjoyed this trip through the rich history of the Bears. We tried to cover it all from the joys of the 1985 season to some of the darker days in the franchise's history.

In the Super Bowl era, Chicago has had its fair share of highlights, but there have been some lean years in the Windy City as well. Throughout the Bears' storied history, some of the best players to ever play the game have come through Halas Hall, which is why the Bears have more Hall-of-Famers than any other team. Chicago might not have the Lombardi Trophies to prove it, but the Bears are a large part of the fabric of the league we know and love.

This book is designed for you, the fans, to be able to embrace your favorite team and feel closer to them. Maybe you weren't familiar with the history of the franchise and were unaware of the early success Chicago had in the NFL.

Perhaps you didn't realize just how shrewdly Chicago traded draft picks in order to pick legendary talents. Or maybe we couldn't stump you at all, and you're the ultimate superfan. No matter how well you did on the quizzes, we hope we captured the spirit of the Bears and inspired even more pride for your team.

The Bears are again searching for a franchise quarterback, a never-ending quest for Chicago's NFL franchise, but the defense is as ferocious as ever with Khalil Mack leading the charge. No matter how well or poorly the Bears play, they will always be at the heart of what makes Chicago special. The Bears are still the winningest team in league history, and they should hold on to that title for the next few years at least. But, as always, they will Bear Down and give it their all.

Made in the USA
Monee, IL
28 May 2023

34860832R00079